The Voodoo Path

Unveiling the Mysteries of New Orleans Voodoo and Haitian Vodou for Spiritual Seekers and Curious Souls

© **Copyright 2024 - All rights reserved.**

The content contained within this book may not be reproduced, duplicated, or transmitted without direct written permission from the author or the publisher.

Under no circumstances will any blame or legal responsibility be held against the publisher, or author, for any damages, reparation, or monetary loss due to the information contained within this book, either directly or indirectly.

Legal Notice:

This book is copyright protected. It is only for personal use. You cannot amend, distribute, sell, use, quote, or paraphrase any part, or the content within this book, without the consent of the author or publisher.

Disclaimer Notice:

Please note the information contained within this document is for educational and entertainment purposes only. All effort has been executed to present accurate, up-to-date, reliable, and complete information. No warranties of any kind are declared or implied. Readers acknowledge that the author is not engaging in the rendering of legal, financial, medical, or professional advice. The content within this book has been derived from various sources. Please consult a licensed professional before attempting any techniques outlined in this book.

By reading this document, the reader agrees that under no circumstances is the author responsible for any losses, direct or indirect, that are incurred as a result of the use of the information contained within this document, including, but not limited to, errors, omissions, or inaccuracies.

Your Free Gift
(only available for a limited time)

Thanks for getting this book! If you want to learn more about various spirituality topics, then join Mari Silva's community and get a free guided meditation MP3 for awakening your third eye. This guided meditation mp3 is designed to open and strengthen ones third eye so you can experience a higher state of consciousness. Simply visit the link below the image to get started.

https://spiritualityspot.com/meditation

Or, Scan the QR code!

Table of Contents

PART 1: VOODOO FOR BEGINNERS 1
   INTRODUCTION 2
   CHAPTER ONE: UNDERSTANDING VOODOO AND HOODOO 4
   CHAPTER TWO: BONDYE AND THE WORLD 13
   CHAPTER THREE: VOODOO ALLIES: THE LWA AND THE
   ANCESTORS 21
   CHAPTER FOUR: THE RADA LWA 30
   CHAPTER FIVE: THE GEDE LWA 40
   CHAPTER SIX: THE PETRO LWA 47
   CHAPTER SEVEN: VOODOO AND HOODOO ALTARS 56
   CHAPTER EIGHT: MOJO BAGS AND GRIS-GRIS 65
   CHAPTER NINE: CLEANSING AND RAISING PROTECTIONS 74
   CHAPTER TEN: VOODOO FOR LOVE AND ABUNDANCE 83
   GLOSSARY 93
   CONCLUSION 101
PART 2: NEW ORLEANS VOODOO 103
   INTRODUCTION 104
   CHAPTER ONE: WHAT MAKES NEW ORLEANS VOODOO
   DIFFERENT? 106
   CHAPTER TWO: GETTING READY FOR VOODOO 116
   CHAPTER THREE: INGREDIENTS AND MATERIALS YOU MIGHT
   NEED 125
   CHAPTER FOUR: BONDYE AND THE LOA PANTHEON 136

CHAPTER FIVE: MAJOR FEMALE LOA 145
CHAPTER SIX: MAJOR MALE LOA 153
CHAPTER SEVEN: CREATING YOUR VOODOO ALTAR 162
CHAPTER EIGHT: YOU AND THE WISDOM OF YOUR
ANCESTORS 170
CHAPTER NINE: VOODOO DOLLS AND CHARMS 178
CHAPTER TEN: VOODOO SPELLS AND RITUALS TO TRY 188
CONCLUSION 201
HERE'S ANOTHER BOOK BY MARI SILVA THAT YOU MIGHT LIKE 203
YOUR FREE GIFT (ONLY AVAILABLE FOR A LIMITED TIME) 204
REFERENCES 205
IMAGE SOURCES 207

Part 1: Voodoo for Beginners

A Guide to New Orleans Voodoo, Haitian Vodou, and Hoodoo

Introduction

The great Maya Angelou once said, *"The more you know of your history, the more liberated you are."* And that is precisely what this book aims to do; to enlighten you about Voodoo's fascinating history, rituals, and practices.

Whether you're a skeptic or a believer, this book is for you if you want to look into the story of Voodoo. From the vibrant streets of New Orleans to the mystical land of Haiti, Voodoo has captivated people's imaginations for centuries. But what exactly is Voodoo? Is it a religion, a culture, a way of life, or something else entirely? These questions will be explored through this book's pages, which will delve into the complex and multifaceted world of Voodoo.

But what sets this book apart from the others on the market? For one, it's written in simple English that's easy to grasp. You'll never find yourself feeling lost about what the concepts within this book are as it leads you through the labyrinthine world of Voodoo.

And that's not all – this book is tailor-made for beginners. You don't need any prior knowledge or experience with Voodoo to pick up this guide and start your journey. The complex and sometimes daunting world of Voodoo has been distilled to leave you with crystal-clear knowledge on the topic.

But this book doesn't just stop at theory. It is also chock-full of hands-on methods and instructions. You'll learn how to create your own Voodoo dolls, cast spells, and perform rituals passed down for generations. With the step-by-step guides, you can practice Voodoo in your home and experience its transformative power for yourself.

As the great detective Sherlock Holmes once said, "It is a capital mistake to theorize before one has data." So, reading this book will provide you with the data you need to fully appreciate and understand the world of Voodoo. Whether you're a curious beginner or a seasoned practitioner, this guide is bound to enrich your knowledge and deepen your understanding of this ancient and mysterious tradition. So, what are you waiting for? Turn the page and begin a journey through the fascinating world of Voodoo.

Chapter One: Understanding Voodoo and Hoodoo

As you delve into the historical and cultural evolution of Haitian Vodou, New Orleans Voodoo, and Hoodoo, you will find a complex web of beliefs and practices intertwined with the experiences of African descendants in the Americas. These practices emerged as a way to preserve and celebrate African spirituality, often in the face of oppressive forces seeking to erase it.

Haitian Vodou

Haitian Vodou is a complex and nuanced spiritual practice that emerged from the experiences of enslaved West Africans in Haiti. The practice is deeply rooted in the traditions of West African spirituality and was further shaped by the forced life of slavery and the resistance of enslaved Africans toward their oppressors. The practice of Vodou began with the arrival of enslaved Africans in Haiti in the 16th century. These individuals came from various West African regions, each with their own spiritual traditions and practices. However, they were all brought together under the brutal living standards of slavery, and these spiritual practices became a way to preserve the slaves' original culture and resist the wishes of their oppressors.

One of the central beliefs of Haitian Vodou is the idea of the Loa, or spirits, who are seen as intermediaries between humans and the divine. The Loa are believed to be able to communicate with the ancestors and offer protection and guidance to those who honor them. Many of the Loa in Haitian Vodou have roots in West African spiritual traditions. Still, they have evolved and been adapted over time to reflect the experiences of Haitians. The practice of Haitian Vodou also includes elements of Catholicism, the dominant religion of the French colonizers in Haiti. The enslaved Africans in Haiti were forced to convert to Catholicism. Still, they often found ways to incorporate their own spiritual practices into the religion. For example, they identified Catholic saints with the Loa and used Catholic symbols and rituals in their Vodou ceremonies.

One of the most important aspects of Haitian Vodou is the role of the priest or priestess, known as the houngan or mambo. These individuals are believed to have a special connection to the Loa. They are responsible for leading ceremonies and performing rituals. The houngan or mambo undergo a period of training and initiation, during which they learn the secrets of Vodou and the ways to communicate with the Loa. The practice of Haitian Vodou has faced persecution and suppression throughout history. The French colonizers in Haiti saw Vodou as threatening their authority and tried to suppress it by force. However, Vodou continued to be practiced in secret, and it played a significant role in the Haitian Revolution, which resulted in Haiti becoming the first black republic in the world.

After the Haitian Revolution, Vodou continued to be practiced in Haiti and spread to other parts of the world. However, it was still viewed with suspicion and fear by many. In the early 20th century, the American journalist William Seabrook authored a sensationalized book about Vodou called "The Magic Island," which perpetuated many negative stereotypes about the practice. Despite these challenges, Haitian Vodou has continued evolving and adapting. Today, it is practiced by millions of people around the world and has had a significant impact on art, music, and literature. Haitian Vodou continues to be a powerful force for spiritual healing and cultural preservation, and it serves as a reminder of the sheer strength of African descendants in the Americas.

New Orleans Voodoo

New Orleans Voodoo, also known as Louisiana Voodoo, is a unique blend of African and European religious and cultural practices and Native American influences. It has been shaped by the history of the city and the people who have called it home. New Orleans Voodoo has its roots in the transatlantic slave trade, which brought millions of Africans to the Americas. Many of these enslaved Africans were from the areas now known as Benin and Togo, where the religion of Vodun (or Voodoo) originated. These Africans were forced to work on plantations in Louisiana, where they were forbidden to practice their own religions. However, they found ways to blend their traditions with those of their captors, resulting in the unique form of Voodoo that is still practiced in New Orleans today.

A Louisiana voodoo altar.[1]

In the late 18th and early 19th centuries, several free people of color in New Orleans began practicing Voodoo openly. These practitioners were often healers and spiritual leaders in their communities, and their influence grew rapidly. They preserved many aspects of the original Vodun religion, including using ritual objects and worshiping ancestral spirits. One of the most well-known figures in the history of New Orleans Voodoo is Marie Laveau. Born in 1801, Laveau was a free woman of color who became a renowned Voodoo priestess. She was known for her healing powers and her ability to communicate with spirits. Laveau was so influential that she was said to have the power to grant or deny favors from the city's politicians.

After the Civil War, the practice of Voodoo began to decline in New Orleans as many African Americans converted to Christianity. However, their religion never completely died out. In the early 20th century, many writers and artists became interested in Voodoo, which began appearing in popular culture. This led to a revival of interest in religion among African Americans, and it has continued to be practiced in New Orleans to this day.

One of the key features of New Orleans Voodoo is its emphasis on personal relationships with spirits. Practitioners believe that spirits can be called upon to help with all manner of problems, from health issues to financial troubles. They also believe in using charms, talismans, and spells to protect themselves and their loved ones from harm. Another important aspect of New Orleans Voodoo is using music and dance in ritual practices. Voodoo ceremonies often involve drumming and chanting. Participants may enter into a trance-like state as they communicate with the spirits.

In recent years, New Orleans Voodoo has faced criticism from some quarters for its association with negative stereotypes, such as the idea of the "Voodoo doll" as a tool for revenge. However, practitioners argue that these stereotypes are based on misunderstanding the religion and its practices. They point out that Voodoo is a deeply spiritual and personal religion and has played an important role in the culture of New Orleans. Its history is intertwined with the city's history, and its traditions have been passed down through generations of practitioners. Whether you are a believer or a skeptic, there is no denying the unique and enduring influence of New Orleans Voodoo on the culture and mythology of America.

Hoodoo

Hoodoo, or *conjure*, is a spiritual practice developed among African Americans in the Southern United States. Its roots can be traced back to West and Central African religious practices brought to America during the transatlantic slave trade. Hoodoo has a complex and varied history, influenced by the traditions of multiple African ethnic groups and Native American and European American folk magic. Because of this, it has developed into a distinct spiritual practice with a unique blend of beliefs, rituals, and practices.

The word "hoodoo" itself is believed to have originated from the term "hudu" or "joodoo," which was used to describe a West African religious practice. Over time, "hoodoo" became a catch-all term for various African American spiritual practices. During the antebellum period, many enslaved Africans were forbidden from practicing their traditional religions. As a result, they adapted their beliefs and practices to fit within the Christian framework imposed upon them by their masters. This led to the development of a form of hoodoo incorporating elements of Christianity, including using the Bible and Christian saints in spells and rituals.

After the Civil War, hoodoo continued to evolve and adapt to the changing social and cultural landscape of the South. It became popular among rural and urban African Americans, and its practices were often passed down through oral tradition within families and communities. Hoodoo practitioners, also known as rootworkers, often created and sold amulets, talismans, and other items believed to have magical properties. They would also perform spells and rituals for clients seeking protection, healing, love, or prosperity.

In addition to its African roots, the practices of Native Americans and Europeans have influenced hoodoo. For example, using herbs and roots in hoodoo can be traced back to the Native American practice of using medicinal plants for healing. Meanwhile, European folk magic, such as using astrology and numerology, has also been incorporated into hoodoo practices. In the early 20th century, hoodoo gained a reputation for being associated with evil or dark magic. This was largely due to negative portrayals in the media and the practice's association with African American culture, often demonized by mainstream society.

Despite this negative perception, hoodoo continued to thrive within African American communities. In the mid-20th century, hoodoo became increasingly popular among white practitioners, particularly in the context of the American folk music revival. This also led to a renewed interest in hoodoo among African Americans, and the practice experienced a revival during the Civil Rights Movement. Hoodoo remains a vibrant and evolving spiritual practice with practitioners worldwide. While many aspects of the practice have changed over time, its core beliefs and values remain rooted in the African American experience and culture. For hoodoo practitioners, freedom is found in the ability to connect with their ancestors, spirits, and the divine and create a better world for themselves and their communities.

All three practices, Haitian Vodou, New Orleans Voodoo, and Hoodoo, have faced persecution and misrepresentation throughout history. They were often viewed as dangerous and were suppressed by the authorities. However, they have endured and evolved, adapting to new circumstances and incorporating new influences. Today, they continue to be practiced by people worldwide who seek a connection to their ancestors, protection from the spirits, and healing for their communities. The evolution of these practices is a testament to the resilience of African spirituality and the importance of preserving cultural traditions. By learning about these practices and understanding their historical and cultural contexts, you can gain a deeper appreciation for the diversity and richness of African spiritual practices and the experiences of African descendants in the Americas.

Similarities and Differences

As you explore the world of Afro-Caribbean religions, it's important to understand the similarities and differences between three distinct practices: Haitian Vodou, New Orleans Voodoo, and Hoodoo. While they share a common history and ancestry, each has its unique identity and beliefs. First, the similarities. All three practices result from the cultural syncretism between African and European traditions that occurred during the transatlantic slave trade. They are all practiced in the Americas and are a blend of West African, Native American, and European spiritual beliefs. The practitioners of all three practices believe in the power of ancestor veneration, divination, and the use of natural elements to effect change in their lives. All three also recognize the importance of spirits, deities, and the unseen world. Haitian Vodou, New Orleans Voodoo, and Hoodoo all utilize herbs, roots, and other natural elements to make medicines, charms, and potions. Each practice also involves using talismans, amulets, and spiritual baths.

Now, what are the differences? Haitian Vodou is an Afro-Haitian religion that emerged in Haiti during the 18th century. New Orleans Voodoo is a form originally developed in the southern United States, particularly in New Orleans. It has its roots in Haitian Vodou but also incorporates elements of Catholicism and Native American spirituality. New Orleans Voodoo also involves ceremonies and rituals, but they are generally less formal than those of Haitian Vodou. It strongly emphasizes ancestor veneration and the use of talismans, such as gris-gris bags, to protect oneself from harm or bring good luck. Hoodoo practitioners often incorporate Christian elements into their practice, such as using psalms and prayers in their spells and rituals. They also place a great deal of emphasis on rootwork, which involves using herbs, minerals, and other natural elements to create charms and potions for various purposes.

Respect These Practices

To approach Voodoo and Hoodoo with the respect they deserve, it is important to recognize their spiritual significance and the cultural traditions that underpin them. This requires an openness to learning and a willingness to engage with the practices thoughtfully and respectfully. One important aspect of this is recognizing the importance of formal initiation in Voodoo and Hoodoo. Initiation is a process by which a person is formally welcomed into a community of practitioners and given access to that community's knowledge and spiritual practices.

In Voodoo, initiation typically involves undergoing a series of rituals and ceremonies, including offerings to the spirits and the performance of divination. The objective of initiation is to establish a relationship between the practitioner and the spirits and to gain a deeper understanding of the spiritual significance of Voodoo. Similarly, in Hoodoo, initiation involves passing knowledge and practices from generation to generation. This can involve learning from a family member or other experienced practitioner and may involve undergoing specific rituals or ceremonies to mark the transition into full membership in the Hoodoo community. Initiation is essential in both Voodoo and Hoodoo because it allows practitioners to fully engage with the spiritual significance of these practices and to understand the deeper meanings behind the rituals and ceremonies they perform.

Another important aspect of approaching Voodoo and Hoodoo respectfully is avoiding whitewashing or appropriating these practices. This means recognizing and honoring the cultural traditions that underpin them and not attempting to strip them of their African roots. For example, in the United States, white practitioners of Hoodoo and Voodoo have long been appropriating these practices and attempting to erase these African roots. This can take many forms, from claiming to have access to secret knowledge or spiritual powers to co-opting symbols and practices from other cultures and presenting them as their own. To avoid this kind of appropriation, it is important to approach Voodoo and Hoodoo with humility and a willingness to learn from those who have practiced these traditions for generations. This may involve seeking out experienced practitioners and learning from them or engaging in serious research to better understand the cultural traditions that underpin these practices.

A Warning

It is important to approach the practice of Voodoo and Hoodoo with great respect and caution. These sacred traditions have been passed down through generations, and it is essential to understand their significance and power before attempting to engage in them. One of the most significant dangers of approaching Voodoo or Hoodoo without proper knowledge or guidance is the risk of invoking spirits inappropriately or disrespectfully. These spirits are not to be taken lightly or used for personal gain, and invoking them without proper preparation and intention can have serious consequences. It is common for those who attempt to practice Voodoo or Hoodoo without the proper knowledge to experience negative - or even dangerous - outcomes.

In many spiritual traditions, the act of invoking spirits is considered to be a powerful and potentially dangerous practice. In Voodoo and Hoodoo, this is no exception. In fact, it is of the utmost importance that anyone seeking to work with spirits in these traditions approaches the practice with respect, caution, and proper guidance. One of the primary risks of invoking spirits without proper initiation or guidance is the potential for harm to oneself or others. Spirits can be powerful entities with their own agendas, and they may not always be benevolent or helpful. If someone attempts to work with a spirit without proper knowledge or guidance, they may inadvertently invite in an evil entity or unintentionally offend one of the spirits, resulting in negative consequences such as illness, bad luck, or even physical harm.

Another risk of working with spirits without proper initiation or guidance is the potential for the practitioner to become unbalanced or unstable. In Voodoo and Hoodoo, there is a strong emphasis on spiritual and emotional balance, and this can be difficult to achieve without proper guidance. Attempting to work with spirits on one's own can result in a practitioner becoming too focused on the spiritual realm to the detriment of their physical and emotional well-being. Additionally, when someone works with spirits without proper initiation or guidance, they risk offending the spirits or the community of practitioners. Voodoo and Hoodoo are not casual spiritual practices. They are deeply rooted in specific cultural and historical contexts and are taken very seriously by those who practice them. Engaging in the practice without proper respect or reverence can be seen as disrespectful or appropriating; this could result in negative consequences both in the spiritual realm and in the wider community.

There have been many instances throughout history of individuals attempting to invoke spirits without proper guidance or initiation, with disastrous results. In some cases, malevolent entities have possessed practitioners, resulting in physical harm or death. In others, individuals have unintentionally offended powerful spirits, resulting in long-term misfortune or illness. In some cases, individuals who have attempted to practice Voodoo or Hoodoo without proper respect have been met with backlash from the wider community of practitioners, resulting in being ostracized or even being subject to violence.

That is why it is strongly advised against invoking any spirits or attempting spells and rituals from what you have heard. Instead, seeking guidance from an experienced practitioner or conducting serious research before practicing these traditions independently is recommended. An experienced practitioner can provide valuable guidance on approaching these practices respectfully. They can also guide you in finding a proper teacher or mentor who can provide further guidance on safely engaging in these traditions. Additionally, reading books or attending classes and workshops can provide a foundation of knowledge and understanding before attempting to practice.

Understanding that these are not mere parlor tricks or entertainment is essential. Voodoo and Hoodoo are serious spiritual practices with a rich cultural history and deep roots in African spirituality. They are not to be taken lightly or treated as a form of entertainment. The best way to approach these practices is with humility and a willingness to learn. It is essential to understand Voodoo and Hoodoo's cultural context and approach them with an open mind and deep respect for the traditions and spirits involved. It is also important to note that formal initiation is recommended in many Voodoo and Hoodoo traditions. Initiation involves a process of spiritual development, where you are taught the proper way to approach the spirits and how to use them in a respectful and responsible way. This is not a process to be taken lightly, as it involves a commitment to the tradition and to the spirits themselves.

Chapter Two: Bondye and the World

The concept of a supreme being is central to many religious and spiritual traditions, and Haitian Vodou, New Orleans Voodoo, and Hoodoo are no exception. In these practices, the Supreme Being is known as Bondye, a deity who is both mysterious and powerful and who is the creator of the universe and all life within it.

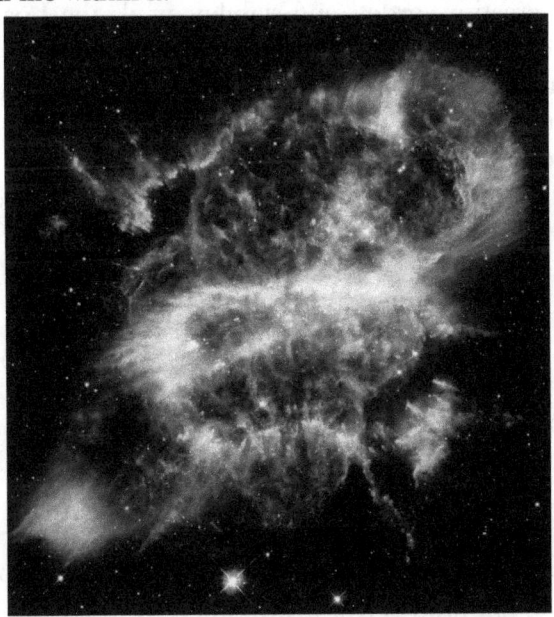

Bondye is the supreme being that created the universe.[2]

On Bondye

Bondye is often described as being beyond human comprehension, existing in a realm beyond our understanding. His name is derived from the French phrase "Bon Dieu," which means "good God." This name is significant because it emphasizes Bondye's benevolent nature and distinguishes him from other spirits who may be more mischievous or malevolent in nature. Bondye represents a key element of Haitian Vodou, New Orleans Voodoo, and Hoodoo and serves as a powerful reminder of the mysteries and wonders of the natural world and our place within it. Bondye is often associated with white, representing purity and transcendence. Some practitioners believe that he is the same as the Christian God, while others see him as a distinct deity with his own characteristics and qualities.

According to Haitian Vodou, Bondye was the creator of the universe and all life within it. He is responsible for the cycles of life and death and is said to be present in every aspect of the natural world. The Loa, or spirits, are said to be intermediaries between Bondye and the physical world, allowing humans to communicate with the divine. Unlike the Loa, who are believed to be spirits of deceased ancestors and other beings, Bondye is seen as a purely divine and unchanging force. He is often associated with creation, order, and stability, while the Loa are associated with change, chaos, and transformation. New Orleans Voodoo and Hoodoo also recognize Bondye as the Supreme Being, but their beliefs and practices may differ in some ways from those of Haitian Vodou. For example, in Hoodoo, Bondye is often seen as less central to the practice than in Haitian Vodou, with greater emphasis placed on the use of herbs, roots, and other natural materials to work magic and influence the world you live in.

Despite these differences, the concept of Bondye as the Supreme Being remains a central part of all three traditions. Bondye is seen as a powerful and benevolent deity who holds the key to the mysteries of the universe and the cycles of life and death which govern this world. In many ways, he can be seen as a symbol of hope and transcendence, offering practitioners of Haitian Vodou, New Orleans Voodoo, and Hoodoo a way to connect with something greater than themselves and find meaning and purpose in a world that often seems chaotic and unpredictable.

At the same time, however, it is important to recognize the limitations of our understanding of Bondye and the spiritual realms which he inhabits. While the Loa may provide a means of communication between humanity and the divine, they are not infallible, and it is always important to approach spiritual practices with respect and caution, seeking guidance from experienced practitioners and doing your own research to deepen your understanding of these complex and powerful traditions.

How Bondye Made the World

The creation of the world is a central theme in the beliefs of many spiritual practices, and Haitian Vodou, New Orleans Voodoo, and Hoodoo are no exception. At the center of these practices is the belief in a supreme being, Bondye, who is credited with creating the world and all that is in it. In Haitian Vodou, Bondye is believed to have created the world through a process involving separating the earth from the sky and creating the first humans from clay. According to Haitian Vodou, the world was created in seven days, with each day representing a different aspect of creation. The first day was dedicated to the creation of the heavens, followed by the creation of the earth, the sea, the sun, the moon, animals, and finally, humans. This process of creation is seen as a reflection of Bondye's power and creativity, as well as symbolizing his ongoing relationship with the world and its inhabitants.

The creation story is slightly different in New Orleans Voodoo, but the basic themes remain the same. According to New Orleans Voodoo, Bondye created the world through a process of division, creating the physical world from a single source of energy. This process of division is seen as a reflection of Bondye's power and creativity and a symbol of his ongoing relationship with the world and its inhabitants.

Hoodoo, on the other hand, does not have a specific creation story. Rather, Hoodoo practitioners believe that the world was created by a combination of natural forces and spiritual energies, with Bondye as the ultimate source of these energies. This belief in a combination of natural and spiritual energies reflects Hoodoo's roots in African traditional religions, which often view the natural and spiritual worlds as interconnected and interdependent.

Despite the differences in their creation stories, all three practices emphasize the central role of Bondye in the creation of the world and the ongoing relationship between the divine and the physical world. This relationship is seen as an essential part of spiritual life, with practitioners often seeking to deepen their connection to Bondye through prayer, meditation, and ritual practice. It is worth noting that the creation stories of these practices are not meant to be taken literally but rather as symbolic representations of the relationship between the divine and the physical world. As with many other spiritual practices, the focus of belief is not on the details of the creation story itself but on the deeper meaning and symbolism behind it.

Haitian Vodou and Bondye

As the Supreme Being, Bondye plays a critical role in Haitian Vodou. Unlike the Lwa (or Loa), who are considered to be more accessible and can be invoked through ritual and prayer, Bondye is often seen as too distant to be directly contacted by human beings. He is a remote and powerful figure and is not typically worshiped in the same way as the Lwa. Instead, Haitian Vodou practitioners view Bondye as a distant observer of the world whose power is felt through his creations, including the Lwa and the natural world.

In Haitian Vodou, the relationship between humans and the divine is mediated through the Lwa, who are seen as the most active force in the universe. While the Lwa can be called upon for specific purposes such as healing, protection, or prosperity, Bondye is seen as the source of all these powers. Because of this, his influence is felt through the Lwa and their actions in the world.

The importance of Bondye in Haitian Vodou is also reflected in the religion's practices and rituals. Bondye is often invoked at the beginning and end of Vodou ceremonies, and his name is often used in blessings and prayers. However, because he is seen as too remote to be directly contacted, he is not typically the focus of Vodou worship. Instead, the Lwa are the main focus of most ceremonies, and it is through their presence that the power of Bondye is felt. One of the most important aspects of Bondye's role in Haitian Vodou is the belief that he is the source of all life and the universe. This story is often retold in Haitian Vodou ceremonies and is central to the religion's beliefs. It emphasizes the interconnectedness of all things and the idea that everything in the world is connected to Bondye, the ultimate source of power and creation.

New Orleans Voodoo and Bondye

In New Orleans Voodoo, Bondye is also recognized as the Supreme Being, but his role is slightly different from how he is seen in Haitian

Vodou. The influence of Catholicism and the cultural context of New Orleans has contributed to the development of a unique form of Vodou emphasizing the intercession of saints and spirits in addition to how practitioners see Bondye. In New Orleans Voodoo, Bondye is often referred to as "Gran Met" or "Great Master" and is seen as the creator of the universe and all living things. Like Haitian Vodou, there is a belief in a dualistic cosmology, with the material and spiritual worlds existing simultaneously but separately. Bondye is seen as the source of all creation and is often depicted as a distant and powerful force. His communication with him is mediated through intermediaries such as spirits and saints.

However, unlike in Haitian Vodou, the spirits or "Lwa" in New Orleans Vodou are often viewed as having more direct influence and power over everyday life. This is due in part to the cultural influence of Louisiana, which has a history of folk practices and syncretism between Catholicism and African spiritual traditions. In New Orleans Voodoo, the spirits are seen as having the ability to intervene in human affairs and provide assistance or protection, and they are often the focus of veneration and ritual practices. Incorporating Catholicism, New Orleans Voodoo also recognizes the importance of saints in the spiritual realm, and many practitioners will invoke Catholic saints alongside the spirits of Vodou. This syncretic approach is also reflected in the use of Catholic iconography in Vodou rituals and the inclusion of elements such as candles and incense in Vodou practices.

Hoodoo and Bondye

In the tradition of Hoodoo, the role of Bondye is somewhat different from the way he is viewed in Haitian and New Orleans Voodoo. Bondye is seen as the ultimate creator and source of all spiritual power, but he is not typically worshiped or invoked directly in Hoodoo practices. Instead, practitioners of Hoodoo often focus on working with individual spirits and spiritual forces to achieve their desired outcomes.

Bondye still plays an important role in Hoodoo as the ultimate source of all spiritual power. Many Hoodoo practitioners believe that all spirits and spiritual forces are ultimately under Bondye's control and can be called upon through the power of his name. In some Hoodoo traditions, the name "Bon Dieu" (meaning "good God" in French, a legacy of Hoodoo's Creole roots) is used as a general term for any divine or spiritual force that can be called upon for assistance.

One of the key differences between Hoodoo and the Vodou traditions is that Hoodoo does not typically involve formal initiation or membership in a specific religious community. Instead, Hoodoo is often passed down through families or acquired through personal study and practice. As a result, depending on their personal beliefs and experiences, individual practitioners may have different views on the role of Bondye and other spiritual forces in their practice. Despite these differences, however, many Hoodoo practitioners still deeply respect Bondye as the ultimate source of all spiritual power. They may use his name in prayers or invocations or may seek to align themselves with his divine will in their magical work. Ultimately, the role of Bondye in Hoodoo is a complex and multifaceted one, reflecting the diverse spiritual beliefs and practices of this unique African American folk tradition.

On the Loa

First, it is essential to understand that the Loa (or Lwa) are not gods in the traditional sense. They are not omnipotent, omnipresent, or omniscient. Instead, they are beings with unique personalities and specific areas of expertise. Each Loa has its own distinct history, mythology, and abilities. Some are associated with particular places, while others are connected to specific aspects of life, such as love, health, or wealth. The Loa are believed to be powerful spiritual entities that can provide guidance, protection, and blessings to those who worship them.

The relationship between Bondye and the Loa is a complex one. Bondye is considered the Supreme Being, the creator of the universe, and the source of all life. The Loa, on the other hand, are seen as intermediaries, bridging the gap between the physical and the spiritual world. They are believed to be the spirits of those who have passed on and are now part of the spiritual realm. Some believe that the Loa were originally humans who achieved a higher spiritual state after death and were elevated to a position of divine influence. Others believe that the Loa are independent spirits that have always existed and were simply acknowledged and incorporated into Vodou practices over time. In either case, it is believed that Bondye gave the Loa their power and authority to interact with humans and affect the physical world. The exact details of how the Loa were created and by whom vary among different Vodou traditions and interpretations.

The Loa work with Bondye to provide spiritual guidance and blessings to practitioners. In Haitian Vodou and New Orleans Voodoo, the Loa are summoned through rituals and ceremonies that involve music, dance, and offerings. Practitioners often make offerings to the Loa, such as food, alcohol, or flowers, to establish a relationship and gain their favor. The Loa are believed to have a particular fondness for certain types of offerings and may be more likely to provide blessings when they are presented with their preferred gifts.

In Hoodoo, the relationship between the Loa and practitioners is less formal. While the Loa are still considered powerful spirits, Hoodoo practitioners may not perform formal ceremonies or make offerings to them. Instead, the Loa may be called upon in spells or rituals to provide guidance or protection. Hoodoo practitioners may also work with other spirits, such as ancestors or guardian angels, in addition to the Loa.

It's important to note that the Loa are not all-powerful. They cannot grant every request, and they may not always answer prayers in the way that practitioners expect. While the Loa are believed to have the power to influence the physical world, they are also subject to the laws of nature and the will of Bondye. Some practitioners may mistakenly assume that the Loa are omnipotent, leading to disappointment or disillusionment when their prayers are not answered as expected.

Additionally, the Loa are often misunderstood as gods or demons by those who are unfamiliar with Haitian Vodou, New Orleans Voodoo, and Hoodoo. This misconception may be partly due to the Loas' powerful abilities and unique personalities. Some Loa are associated with darker aspects of life, such as death or disease, which may contribute to the idea that they are malevolent beings. However, this is a misunderstanding of their role in these practices. The Loa are not worshiped in the same way as gods or demons and are not seen as being fundamentally different from human beings. Instead, they are considered to be part of the spiritual realm, just like ancestors and guardian angels.

Please don't attempt to go directly to Bondye. Bondye is considered too powerful and too remote for most humans to communicate effectively, making direct communication difficult, if not impossible. Don't take this to mean that the good God doesn't care about you and your affairs. He does, and that's why he has sent intermediaries so you can communicate with each other through them. Also, trying to invoke him would be disrespectful to all Vodou practices. If you consider that your problem is so urgent that only Bondye can help, it is recommended that you seek the guidance of an experienced practitioner of Vodou, who can help you to communicate with the divine in a safe and effective way. This may involve ritual purification, offerings to the Loa, and the guidance of an intermediary who is experienced in communicating with the divine.

Chapter Three: Voodoo Allies: The Lwa and the Ancestors

The Lwa, or Loa, are spirits who play a significant role in the African diasporic religion of Voodoo. In Haitian Voodoo, the Lwa are organized into seven "nanchons" or "nations," each with its own characteristics, symbols, and rituals. Understanding the nature of each nanchon is important for Voodoo practitioners, as it guides the selection of appropriate offerings, songs, and dances to invoke the Lwa. In New Orleans Voodoo, there are only three nanchons: The Rada, Petro, and Gede nanchons. As for Hoodoo, there isn't a lot of emphasis placed on the classifications of these spirits.

The Lwa or Loa are spirits that play an important role in Voodoo.[8]

The Haitian Vodou Nanchons

The Rada Lwa: The first nanchon is Rada, also known as Radha. The Rada Lwa are considered to be the oldest of the seven nations of Lwa and are associated with the spirits of the Fon people of Dahomey. Their traditions emphasize harmony, peace, and healing. The Rada Lwa are often called upon to resolve conflicts, heal illnesses, and bring prosperity to their followers. The symbols associated with the Rada Lwa are generally round and symmetrical, and their veves often include circles and intersecting lines. The Rada Lwa are often invoked through drumming and dancing, as well as through the use of specific herbal remedies and spiritual baths. Followers of the Rada tradition may also offer gifts and sacrifices to the Lwa, such as food, drink, and animal sacrifices.

The Petro Lwa: The second nanchon is Petro, also known as Pethro or Petwo. These fierce and fiery entities have a reputation for being some of the most dangerous and unpredictable in the Vodou religion. The Petro Lwa are associated with the spirits of the Haitian Revolution, and their traditions emphasize power, resistance, and revolution. These spirits are often called upon to help their followers fight against oppression and injustice, and they are known for their ability to unleash powerful forces of destruction against their enemies. The symbols associated with the Petro Lwa are generally jagged and asymmetrical, and their veves often include zig-zags and sharp angles.

The spirits in this nation are also known for their association with fire and blood. These powerful forces are believed to be the key to unlocking the full potential of the Petro Lwa, and many of their rituals involve the use of fire and blood to activate their powers. However, the power of the Petro Lwa is not without its risks. These spirits are known for their volatile and unpredictable nature, and they are not to be trifled with. Those seeking to work with the Petro Lwa must approach with caution and respect and be prepared to deal with the consequences of their actions.

Furthermore, the Petro Lwa are often misunderstood and maligned by those outside of the Vodou community. They are sometimes associated with dark magic and evil forces, and their followers are often demonized and persecuted. This is a tragic misunderstanding of the true nature of the Petro Lwa, and it highlights the importance of education and understanding when it comes to the Vodou religion.

The Nago Lwa: The Nago nation of Lwa is a group of spirits deeply rooted in the African Yoruba religion. They are known for their fierce and warrior-like qualities. They are often called upon to help with matters related to protection, justice, and strength. It is said that the Nago Lwa possess a deep and intimate knowledge of the secrets of the universe and that they hold the keys to unlocking the mysteries of life and death. The veves associated with this nanchon of Lwa are intricate and complex, often featuring patterns of interlocking lines and geometric shapes. These symbols are thought to represent the complex and intertwined nature of the universe and the interconnectedness of all living things.

In the Vodou tradition, the Nago Lwa are associated with the color red, which is said to represent their fiery and passionate nature. They are often depicted with weapons or symbols of war, such as spears or swords, and are known for their fierce and uncompromising nature. However, despite their warrior-like qualities, these Lwa are also deeply compassionate and caring. Known for their ability to heal, both physically and spiritually, they are often called upon to help those who are suffering from a specific illness or emotional distress. The Lwa are also associated with the element of fire, which is seen as a purifying and transformative force. They are said to have the power to burn away negative energies and help those who seek guidance to rise from the ashes of their past and be reborn anew.

To approach the Nago Lwa is to enter into a world of mystery and power, where the boundaries between the physical and spiritual realms blur and dissolve. Those who seek their guidance must do so with respect and reverence, for the Nago Lwa are not to be trifled with. Despite their fearsome reputation, the Nago Lwa are deeply committed to helping those who seek their guidance. They are known for their fierce loyalty and unwavering dedication to their followers and will go to great lengths to ensure that those seeking their aid are protected and supported.

The Kongo Lwa: The Kongo nanchon of Lwa is a powerful force in the world of Voodoo. Their traditions are deeply rooted in the culture and history of the people of the Kongo taken to Haiti as slaves. The Kongo Lwa are associated with the spirits of the Kongo people, and their traditions emphasize strength, courage, and resilience. They are often called upon to help their followers overcome obstacles and find success in difficult circumstances.

The Kongo Lwa are organized into four families or groups: Lemba, Simbi, Mayisi, and Ti-Jean Petro. Each family has its own set of spirits and traditions, but they are all united by a deep sense of pride and a fierce devotion to their followers. The Lemba family is perhaps the most well-known of the Kongo nanchon. They are associated with the spirits of the royal court of the Kongo kingdom, and their traditions emphasize justice, order, and stability. The Lemba Lwa are often called upon to help resolve disputes and bring peace to their followers. Their veves are often very detailed and intricate, featuring complex geometric patterns and interlocking shapes.

The Simbi family is associated with the spirits of the water, and their traditions emphasize healing and transformation. The Simbi Lwa are often called upon to help heal physical and emotional ailments and to bring about positive changes in their followers' lives. Their veves often feature images of snakes and other water creatures, as well as flowing lines and curves. The Mayisi family is associated with the spirits of the forest, and their traditions emphasize protection and strength. The Mayisi Lwa are often called upon to help their followers overcome obstacles and defend themselves against harm. Their veves often feature images of trees, animals, and other symbols of the forest.

Finally, the Ti-Jean Petro family is associated with the spirits of the Earth, and their traditions emphasize power and transformation. The Ti-Jean Petro Lwa are often called upon to help their followers achieve their goals and overcome their fears. Their veves are often very bold and dramatic, featuring powerful images of fire and earth.

The Djouba Lwa: The fifth nanchon is Djouba, which is associated with the spirits of the Mandinga people of West Africa. The Djouba Lwa are known for their energy and vitality, and they are often called upon to help with fertility, creativity, and inspiration. The Djouba Lwa are also associated with the sun's power and are sometimes invoked to bring light and warmth to their followers. The symbols associated with the Djouba Lwa often include circles, spirals, and sunbursts.

The Djouba nanchon of Lwa, a powerful and enigmatic force within the voodoo religion, embodies a complex web of influences and traditions that span both time and space.

But despite their elusive and often otherworldly nature, the Djouba remain an essential part of voodoo practice, revered for their ability to bring prosperity, good luck, and healing to those who call upon them. One of the most powerful symbols associated with the Djouba nanchon is the crossroads, which represents the intersection of different worlds and the possibility of new beginnings. It is believed that the Djouba Lwa inhabit the crossroads, guiding and protecting those who seek their help.

But the Djouba are not simply passive guardians of the crossroads. They are also active agents of change and transformation, capable of bringing about profound shifts in the lives of their followers. Through their rituals and offerings, the Djouba can heal illness, bring good fortune, and even help to find love. Yet, despite their many gifts and powers, the Djouba nanchon remains a mystery to many outsiders, their true nature and significance known only to those who have earned their trust and respect. To the uninitiated, the Djouba may seem capricious and unpredictable, and their actions and desires difficult to understand.

However, for those who have experienced the transformative power of the Djouba, there is no doubt that these Lwa are a force to be reckoned with as agents of change and transformation who hold the key to unlocking new possibilities and potential. In many ways, the Djouba nanchon embodies the spirit of Voodoo itself, a complex and dynamic tradition that draws upon the wisdom and knowledge of many different cultures and traditions. Like the Lwa themselves, voodoo is a force that transcends boundaries, connecting people across time and space and helping them to navigate the challenges and opportunities of life.

The Ibo Lwa: The sixth nanchon is Ibo, which is associated with the spirits of the Igbo people of Nigeria. The Ibo Lwa are known for their ability to communicate with the spiritual realm, and they are often called upon to help with divination and prophecy. The Ibo Lwa are also associated with the power of the wind, and they are sometimes invoked to bring change and transformation.

The Ibo Lwa are known for their deep connection to nature, drawing inspiration from the earth, the sky, and the spirits that dwell within them. They are fierce protectors of their followers, shielding them from harm and guiding them toward the path of righteousness. Their veves are intricate and complex, depicting the intricate balance between the natural world and the spiritual realm. The Ibo Lwa are often called upon for matters related to justice and morality, and they hold a special place in the hearts of those who seek guidance in times of trouble.

But their power does not come without sacrifice. The Ibo people have faced countless hardships throughout their history, from the horrors of slavery to the brutal colonization of their land. And yet, through it all, they have persevered, holding onto their traditions and their connection to the spirits that guide them. The Ibo Lwa reflect this perseverance, embodying the strength and determination of their people. Their rituals are steeped in tradition, each one carefully crafted to honor the spirits and invoke their power. The rhythms of the drums and the sway of the dancers serve as a conduit, channeling the energy of the spirits and bringing it into the world.

The Ibo Lwa are also associated with the power of knowledge and education. They understand that true power comes not only from physical strength but from the strength of the mind and the wisdom of the soul. They are teachers and guides, imparting their knowledge to those who seek it and helping them to grow and evolve.

The Ghede Lwa: The Ghede nanchon of Lwa is a mysterious and powerful group of spirits known for their connection to death and the afterlife. They are both feared and revered, and their presence is felt throughout the Vodou religion. They are often called upon to help with matters related to death, and their traditions emphasize humor, sexuality, and fertility. In the world of Vodou, they are gatekeepers, holding the key to the mysteries of life and death.

There is a certain mystique surrounding the Ghede nanchon. They are considered outsiders, and their traditions are often misunderstood by those who have little knowledge of the religion. But for those who practice Vodou, the Ghede Lwa is essential to the spiritual landscape. They are a reminder of the fragility of life and the importance of honoring those who have passed on. This nanchon is made up of a diverse group of spirits, each with its own unique attributes and personalities. Some are known for their raucous behavior, while others are more serious and contemplative. But all of them share a deep connection to death and a powerful ability to help guide the souls of the departed.

The Ghede nanchon is also home to many important spirits, each with its own unique personality and role within the nanchon. But despite their differences, they all share a deep connection to the world of the dead and a powerful ability to help those who are struggling with issues related to death and the afterlife. This nanchon is often seen as a symbol of the circle of life; it is a reminder that death is not an end but rather a transition to a new phase of existence. The Ghede Lwa are seen as guides, helping ease the passage of the soul from the physical world to the world beyond.

They also remind one and all of the importance of living life to the fullest. They are known for their raucous celebrations and their love of dance, music, and sex. The Ghede Lwa are a reminder that life is short and that it should be lived with joy and passion. In many ways, they embody the contradictions that are at the heart of the Vodou religion. They are both serious and irreverent, powerful and playful, revered and feared.

On Veves

A "veve" is a symbolic design or drawing representing a specific Lwa or spirit. These intricate designs are created using a variety of materials, including cornmeal, flour, and ashes, and are typically drawn on the ground or on a piece of cloth or paper. The creation of a veve is an important part of invoking a particular Lwa and inviting their presence into a ceremony or ritual. The importance of veves lies in their ability to create a visual connection between the practitioner and the Lwa. Each veve is unique and has specific symbols and patterns corresponding to the attributes and qualities of a particular spirit. For example, the veve for the Lwa Legba (associated with communication and gatekeeping) often includes keys or a crossroads.

When a veve is created, it is accompanied by prayers, chants, and offerings to the Lwa, all of which serve to amplify the practitioner's intent and focus their energy on a specific outcome. Through this process, the veve becomes a powerful tool to invoke the spirit and open up a channel for communication and exchange. However, it is important to note that the use of veves is not a casual or frivolous practice. In recent years, there has been an increase in the mindless use of veves in popular culture, with people tattooing them on their bodies without a clear understanding of their significance or the traditions they are connected to. This trend has led to concerns about cultural appropriation and the commodification of Vodou practices.

Using veves requires respect and understanding of their cultural and spiritual significance. Practitioners must approach the creation and use of veves with clear intent and a deep reverence for the Lwa they represent. This means taking the time to learn about the specific meanings and associations of each veve and understanding the proper protocols for invoking and working with the associated spirit. If you don't use these symbols respectfully, the Lwa may choose to ignore you permanently, or the moodier spirits may punish you for insulting them with your careless use of their symbol. Please understand that veves are not simply decorative designs or symbols to be used for personal gain. They are powerful tools for spiritual transformation and must be used with the utmost care and respect. Veves should only be created and used by those who have undergone proper training and initiation in Vodou traditions and have a deep understanding of the spiritual dimensions of their work.

Your Ancestors

In the vast realm of Voodoo and Hoodoo practices, one cannot overstate the importance of ancestors. The revered ones who have passed before us carry with them the wisdom of the ages, the knowledge of the mysteries of the universe, and the accumulated experiences of their lives. They are the guardians of our lineages, the keepers of your heritage, and the spirits who can guide you toward your destiny. The ancestors are considered the first line of defense, the first point of contact, and the first bridge between the human and the spirit world. They serve as a conduit for the Lwa and are believed to be able to communicate with the ancestors. Thus, invoking the help of the ancestors is a crucial step in any Voodoo or Hoodoo practice.

These spirits are vital because they can offer guidance, protection, and healing. They can also provide spiritual nourishment, blessings, and abundance. They are believed to be able to intervene in the lives of their descendants, particularly in times of need, crisis, or danger. They can help practitioners overcome obstacles, break curses, and succeed in their endeavors.

Contacting Your Ancestors

To contact your ancestors, you must set up an ancestor altar, which can be a simple or elaborate arrangement of photographs, candles, flowers, and offerings. You can then light candles and incense, offer food, drink, or tobacco, and meditate or pray in front of the altar. The goal is to create a sacred space where the ancestors can feel welcomed and honored and where you can communicate with them.

As a beginner Voodooist, you should establish a connection with your ancestors before you attempt to contact the Lwa directly. This is because the ancestors are considered the gateway to the spirit world and can help you navigate the complexities of Voodoo and Hoodoo practices. By establishing a relationship with your ancestors, you can better understand your roots, your lineage, and your place in the world. Your ancestors can also be a source of inspiration, creativity, and intuition. They can guide you toward your purpose, calling, and destiny.

You can access the collective wisdom of your ancestors through your community, culture, and traditions. The ancestors can even help you develop your psychic abilities, divination skills, and other spiritual gifts. However, it is essential to approach the ancestors with respect, humility, and sincerity. They are not to be taken lightly, for they are powerful spirits who demand reverence and gratitude. The ancestors must be honored, fed, and regularly remembered, for they are the foundation of our lives and the guardians of our spirits.

Chapter Four: The Rada Lwa

This chapter teaches you about the cool and gentle Rada spirits. These spirits are beginner-friendly, more so than their fiery and unpredictable Petro counterparts.

Ezili Freda

Ezili Freda is a graceful and elegant Lwa, a divine spirit of love, beauty, femininity, and luxury. She is often depicted as a beautiful woman dressed in white, adorned with pearls, and holding a fan or a mirror. Her presence is calming and soothing, and her energy is nurturing and powerful. Her veve, a sacred symbol used to invoke her presence, is intricately designed with a central heart and feathers, flowers, and other symbols of beauty surrounding it. White and other pastel shades (like pink and blue) are often associated with her. She is also associated with the fragrance of jasmine and other sweet-scented flowers.

In Haitian Vodou, Ezili Freda is syncretized with the Catholic saint, Our Lady of Lourdes; she is often called upon for healing and comfort. She is associated with the concept of pure, unconditional love and is revered for her ability to bring harmony and balance to relationships. She is often paired with the powerful and virile Lwa, Damballa, and together they represent the divine union of male and female energy. She is also associated with other gentle and loving Lwa like Agwe, LaSiren, and Loco.

Ezili Freda is syncretized with Our Lady of Lourdes.'

Lore surrounding Ezili Freda often depicts her as a beautiful and vain woman who enjoys luxury and the finer things in life. She is known for her love of pearls and other precious jewels, and offerings of these items are often made to her. She is also known for her gentle nature and ability to soothe troubled hearts and bring peace to difficult situations. To honor Ezili Freda, practitioners often offer her gifts of champagne, white flowers, and sweets. It is said that if she accepts an offering, she will leave a sign such as the presence of a butterfly, a scent of perfume, or a feeling of calm and love.

Ezili Freda is honored during Carnival season with the Krewe of Muses parade, which features her as their patron Lwa. Mardi Gras Indians also honor her with their elaborate beadwork and feathered costumes. Ezili Freda is a beloved and powerful Lwa who offers guidance, love, and protection to those seeking her out. Her energy is a reminder of the power of love and the beauty of the divine feminine.

There are many real-life stories of individuals who have established a deep and meaningful connection with Ezili Freda. One such story is that of Marie, a young woman from New Orleans. Marie had always been drawn to the spiritual traditions of her ancestors, but it wasn't until she discovered the practice of Vodou that she truly found a sense of belonging. From the moment she first saw Ezili Freda's veve, Marie knew that she had found her spiritual home.

Over time, Marie began to incorporate the veneration of Ezili Freda into her daily practice. She would light candles and offer flowers and other gifts to the spirit, always with a sense of deep reverence and respect.

One day, Marie received a powerful sign that her offerings had been accepted by Ezili Freda. She was walking down the street when she saw a butterfly, its wings the same shade of pink as the flowers she had offered to the spirit earlier that day. As she watched, the butterfly landed on her shoulder and remained there for several minutes before flying away. From that moment on, Marie knew she had a special connection with Ezili Freda. She continued to offer gifts and revere the spirit. In return, she felt a sense of love and protection she had never experienced.

Agwe

Agwe, the ruler of the seas and oceans, is a majestic and powerful Lwa revered by many in the Voodoo and Hoodoo traditions. He is often depicted as a handsome and muscular man with green scales and a mermaid tail, reflecting his association with water. His veve is an intricate symbol of a ship with sails, surrounded by waves and fish, representing his dominion over the seas. Other symbols associated with him include sea shells, coral, and fish hooks.

Agwe is the ruler of the seas.⁵

In the syncretic tradition of Haitian Vodou, Agwe is often associated with the Catholic saint, St. Ulrich, who is also associated with the sea. This syncretism highlights the complex interweaving of African and European traditions that characterize Voodoo and Hoodoo traditions. Agwe's correspondences include the colors blue and green and plants and herbs associated with the ocean, such as seaweed and sea salt. He is also associated with rum, a popular offering to him. He shares close ties with La Sirène and Simbi Andezo.

Agwe is a fierce and protective spirit, willing to do whatever it takes to protect his devotees. He is known to be generous and kind – but also powerful and dangerous when angered. Offerings to Agwe often take the form of food, drink, and other gifts left at the shore or tossed into the sea. Signs that he has received and accepted one's offerings may include calm waters, a successful fishing trip, or other signs of good fortune on the water. Agwe is often celebrated and honored in various ways, including through rituals and offerings at the shore or other bodies of water. The Krewe of Proteus, a Mardi Gras organization founded in 1882, has chosen Agwe as its official patron, reflecting the enduring popularity of this powerful and beloved Lwa in the city's cultural traditions.

Legba

Legba, the guardian of the crossroads, is one of the most important and beloved Lwa in the Voodoo pantheon. He is a wise and mischievous old man, often depicted with a staff and a straw hat, and is known to speak in riddles and cryptic messages. His veve is a simple yet powerful symbol, consisting of a crossroads with a circle at the center. His colors are red and black, and his correspondences include tobacco, rum, and palm oil. He is associated with the herb rue and the plant hibiscus and is syncretized with Saint Peter in the Catholic tradition.

A statue of Legba, the gatekeeper between the human and spirit worlds.[6]

Legba is closely linked with other Lwa, such as Papa Ghede and Baron Samedi, and is said to be the gatekeeper between the human and spirit worlds. He is also known for removing obstacles and providing opportunities, making him a popular choice for those seeking guidance and luck. Often portrayed as a trickster, he uses wit and humor to teach important lessons and keep people on their toes. He is a protector of children and the elderly and revered for his wisdom and ability to see everything.

To honor Legba, offerings of rum, tobacco, and food are often given at crossroads, and his veve is drawn in powdered cornmeal or flour. Signs that he has accepted an offering may include a sudden gust of wind, the sound of footsteps, or the appearance of a stray dog. Legba is celebrated during the annual Voodoo Fest, as well as during Mardi Gras and other festivities. His presence can be felt throughout the city in the music, the food, and the spirit of its people. Legba is a wise and trusted friend for those seeking his guidance and protection.

Loco

Loco is a figure of tremendous strength and vitality, able to move mountains and stir up mighty storms. Often depicted as a tall and muscular man with a fierce and commanding presence, his face is adorned with intricate tribal markings, and his eyes shine with a fierce and unyielding light. He holds a staff of pure gold in his hands, symbolizing his strength and dominion over the elements. One of the most striking symbols associated with Loco is his veve, a powerful and intricate design that represents his presence and power. The veve of Loco features a series of concentric circles, each containing a different symbol or image that represents some aspect of his essence.

In the syncretic traditions of New Orleans, Loco is often associated with the Catholic Saint Anthony of Padua. This connection reflects Loco's role as a guide and protector of the downtrodden and marginalized and his reputation as a miraculous healer and provider of sustenance. In terms of correspondence, Loco is often associated with the color green and various herbs and plants such as mint, basil, and vervain. These correspondences reflect his connection to the natural world and his ability to channel its energies to achieve his goals.

The veve of Loco.[7]

In terms of his relations with other Loa, Loco is often depicted as a powerful ally of Damballa, the serpent spirit of creation, as well as with other figures associated with the natural world, such as Oya and Oshun. He is also said to be fiercely protective of his followers and is not afraid to act against those who seek to harm them. Loco is often depicted as a spirit of great power and mystery, capable of performing miraculous feats and providing guidance and support to those in need. He is also said to possess a fiercely independent streak and is not afraid to challenge authority or convention in pursuit of his goals. Preferred offerings to Loco may include items such as cigars, rum, and other potent spirits, as well as various food items such as chicken, fish, and rice. Signs that Loco has received and accepted one's offerings may include sudden shifts in the weather or the appearance of various animals such as snakes, lizards, or other creatures associated with the natural world.

This Loa is celebrated and honored during various festivals and observances throughout the year, particularly during the annual Mardi Gras celebrations. During these events, offerings are made to Loco to seek his protection and guidance, and various rituals and ceremonies are performed to honor his power and influence.

Damballa

Damballa, the serpent spirit, is a powerful Loa of Haitian Vodou. He is often depicted as a giant white serpent coiled around a staff or as a rainbow. Damballa is associated with creation, wisdom, and the primal forces of the universe. His symbol, the veve, is a stylized representation of a serpent. In Haitian Vodou, this Loa is often syncretized with Saint Patrick, the patron saint of Ireland. His correspondences include the color white, the herb basil, and the plant hibiscus. Damballa is closely associated with his consort, Ayida-Weddo, the rainbow serpent. Together, they represent the universe's balance of masculine and feminine energies. Damballa is also associated with other powerful Loa, such as Papa Legba and Baron Samedi.

Damballa, the serpent spirit.[9]

Lore connected to Damballa depicts him as a wise, benevolent spirit willing to guide and protect his devotees. He is known to be a powerful healer and is often called upon to cure illness or to provide guidance in matters of wisdom and knowledge. Devotees often offer him eggs, milk, and white rum as offerings, which are placed at his altar. Signs that he has received and accepted an offering include the appearance of snakes in the area or the sound of hissing. Damballa is celebrated and honored during various Voodoo ceremonies throughout the year, including the Feast of St. John and the Festival of the Dead. During these celebrations, offerings are given, and prayers are made to Damballa, and his powerful presence is felt by those who attend.

Ayizan

Ayizan is a powerful Loa in the Vodou tradition, known for her ability to connect individuals with the divine and spiritual world. She is often depicted as an elderly woman dressed in white or blue and adorned with cowrie shells and a broom, which symbolize her role as the temple keeper. Her veve, or sacred symbol, is a cross with a horizontal line at the top, and it is often drawn in white or blue on the ground during Vodou ceremonies. Other symbols associated with Ayizan include the broom, cowrie shells, and the acacia tree.

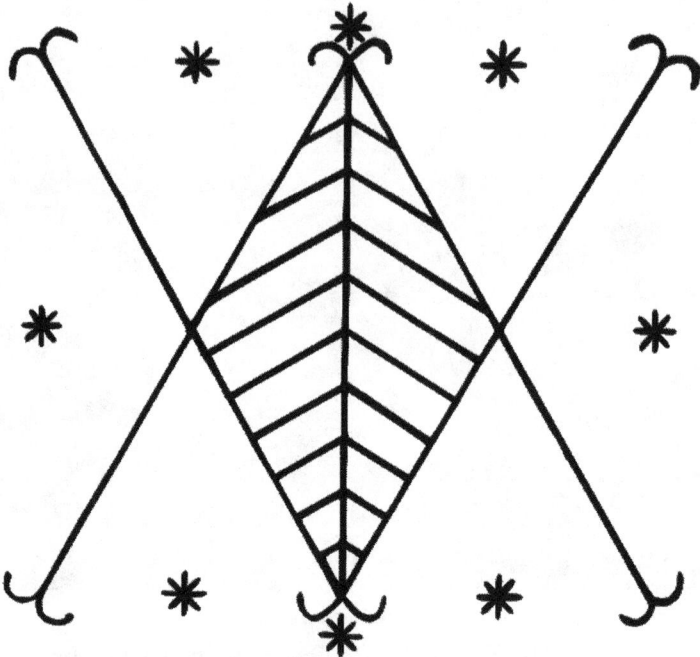

The veve for Ayizan.[9]

Ayizan is sometimes syncretized with the Catholic saint, Our Lady of Mount Carmel, who is also associated with brooms and spiritual cleansing. Her correspondences include the colors white and blue, as well as herbs like rosemary, basil, and lavender. In Vodou, she is often called upon to open the door between the physical and spiritual worlds, allowing for communication with the divine. She is also associated with fertility, healing, and protection and is said to possess a kind and nurturing personality.

According to lore, Ayizan was the first Mambo, or priestess, in the Vodou tradition. She taught others how to communicate with the Loa and was instrumental in spreading the practice throughout Haiti and beyond. Offerings to her often include items such as white candles, brooms, and cowrie shells, as well as food and drink like cornmeal, water, and rum. Signs that Ayizan has received and accepted an offering may include the sound of a broom sweeping the floor or a feeling of spiritual clarity and connection. Ayizan is often celebrated and honored as part of the Vodou tradition, particularly during the annual Voodoo Fest in October. She is also revered by many in the Haitian community, who continue to practice the ancient traditions she helped establish so long ago.

Chapter Five: The Gede Lwa

In this chapter, you'll learn about the most popular Gede Lwa, starting with Baron Samedi.

Baron Samedi

Baron Samedi, the Lord of the Dead, is a complex and multifaceted Loa in the Haitian Vodou tradition. His image is that of a tall, thin man with sunken eyes and a skull-like face. He wears a top hat and a long black coat and is often seen carrying a cane. Despite his fearsome appearance, he is known to be a jovial and charming spirit with a deep sense of humor and a love of life. The veve of Baron Samedi is a simple design consisting of a cross with two small vertical lines on either side. He is also associated with the image of a skull and crossbones, representing his role as the ruler of the dead. In Haitian Vodou, Baron Samedi is syncretized with Saint Martin de Porres, a Peruvian lay brother known for his healing powers and devotion to the poor and the sick.

Baron Samedi, the Loa of death.[10]

Baron Samedi is closely associated with death but also with fertility and rebirth. His colors are black and purple, and his correspondences include tobacco, rum, and coffee. He is often invoked to help with matters related to love and fertility, as well as for protection and healing. In Haitian Vodou, Baron Samedi is considered the leader of the Gede, a group of Loa associated with death and the afterlife. He is married to the powerful Loa Maman Brigitte and is often seen in the company of other Gede spirits, such as Baron La Croix and Baron Kriminel.

Despite his macabre image, Baron Samedi is a beloved and respected figure in Haitian Vodou, known for his wisdom, wit, and ability to help those in need. Devotees of Baron Samedi offer him offerings of tobacco, rum, and other items associated with death and the afterlife. Signs that he has accepted an offering may include the appearance of a black butterfly or the scent of tobacco smoke. Baron Samedi is celebrated as part of the annual Voodoo Festival, which takes place each year in October. Devotees of Vodou honor him by leaving offerings at his altar, dancing and singing in his honor, and participating in rituals and ceremonies designed to honor his power and influence.

Maman Brigitte

Maman Brigitte is a powerful Lwa in the Vodou pantheon with a voice like molasses and a presence like thunder. She is often depicted as a tall, striking woman with fiery red hair and piercing green eyes. She wears a long, flowing dress and carries a machete or a bottle of rum. Her veve is a cross with a circle in the center, and her associated symbols include black roosters, red and black candles, and hot peppers.

In Haitian Vodou, Maman Brigitte is syncretized with the Catholic saint Brigid and is often called upon for protection, justice, and healing. She is associated with death, the afterlife, healing, and transformation. Her colors are black and purple, and her corresponding herbs include basil, bay leaf, and rosemary.

Maman Brigitte is said to have a close relationship with Baron Samedi, the Lwa of death, and is often seen as his wife or sister. She is also associated with the Ghede, a group of Lwa who are the spirits of the dead. She is known for her fierce, protective nature and ability to help those in trouble or facing difficult situations. She is also said to have a mischievous side and enjoys playing pranks on those who do not show her proper respect. Maman Brigitte is a fierce warrior and protector of women. She is also renowned for her love of rum and tobacco, and offerings of these items are said to please her.

Other offerings that are said to please her include black roosters, hot peppers, and red and black candles. Maman Brigitte is celebrated in Haitian Vodou during the Festival of the Dead, which takes place in November. She is honored during the Vodou-inspired Mardi Gras celebrations and the Day of the Dead festivities. She is often invoked for protection and healing, as well as for guidance and strength during times of difficulty. Her presence is felt in the fiery energy of New Orleans, and she is often called upon for her powerful and protective energy.

Baron La Croix

Baron La Croix is one of the lesser-known Loa in the Vodou pantheon, but he is no less powerful or revered. He is often depicted as a man with a fierce countenance dressed in black and white and carrying a walking stick. His veve is a complex pattern of intersecting lines and shapes, often incorporating the colors black, white, and red. This Baron is not syncretized with any Catholic saint, but he does have correspondences to various colors, herbs, and plants. He is associated with black, which represents death and the underworld. Some of the herbs and plants associated with him include horehound, rue, and tobacco.

Baron La Croix has a unique relationship with the other Loa. He is often considered a solitary figure, rarely interacting with other spirits. However, he is sometimes invoked with other Loa, especially those associated with death and the underworld, such as Baron Samedi and Maman Brigitte. There is not much lore surrounding Baron La Croix, but those who have worked with him describe him as a powerful and mysterious force. He is said to be a master of transformation and can help those who seek to change their lives in significant ways.

Preferred offerings for Baron La Croix include rum, cigars, and black candles. Signs that he has received and accepted an offering may include mysterious coincidences, vivid dreams, or a sense of closure or completion. He is not widely celebrated or honored, but some practitioners of Vodou may include him in their personal spiritual practices. He is considered a potent and enigmatic force to be approached with caution and respect.

Baron Cimetière

In Haitian Vodou, Baron Cimetière is often depicted as a skeletal figure wearing a top hat and carrying a cane or a shovel. He is associated with death, cemeteries, and the spirits of the dead. He is also considered to be the guardian of the cemetery and the gatekeeper between the living and the dead. His veve depicts a skull with crossed bones; his colors are black and purple. His offerings include rum, cigars, and black coffee, and his sacred herbs include rue, basil, and lavender. If he seems similar to Baron Samedi, that's because he is another aspect of that Gede Lwa.

Baron Cimetière has strong relationships with other spirits of death and the dead, including Papa Ghede and Maman Brigitte. He is also associated with the Catholic saint, Saint Expeditus, and syncretized with him in some traditions. Regarding lore, the Baron is said to be feared and respected by those working with him. He is known for his blunt and direct manner of speaking and ability to cut through pretense and reveal the truth. He is also believed to be able to impart wisdom and guidance to those who seek his counsel. Baron Cimetière is honored during the Festival of the Dead in Haiti, which takes place in November. In New Orleans Voodoo, he is also celebrated during this time and during the annual Day of the Dead festivities in early November. At these events, offerings of rum, cigars, and black coffee are typically made to honor him, and his veve is often drawn on the ground or on a ceremonial altar.

Gede Nibo

Gede Nibo, the Loa of death and fertility in the Vodou tradition. Gede Nibo is a powerful and mischievous spirit with a sharp wit and a penchant for ribald humor. In the Vodou tradition, Nibo is often depicted as a skeletal figure adorned with a top hat, a black coat, a staff, and medicinal white rum. He is effeminate, too, frequently smoking a cigar. His veve, or sacred symbol, is a series of interconnected triangles representing the crossroads between life and death. Other symbols associated with this Lwa include coffins, bones, and the colors black and purple.

In Haitian Vodou, Gede Nibo is often syncretized with Saint Gerard Majella, a Christian saint known for bringing quick solutions to problems. In New Orleans Voodoo, Gede Nibo is often syncretized with Saint Martin de Porres, a Catholic saint known for his work with the poor and the sick. His correspondences include black and purple and the herbs basil, wormwood, and sage. He is often associated with cemeteries and crossroads and is said to have the power to bring fertility to those who honor him.

In the Vodou pantheon, Gede Nibo is closely related to the other Loa of death and the afterlife, including Baron Samedi and Maman Brigitte. He is also known for his close relationship with Papa Legba (the Loa), the gatekeeper between the mortal and spirit worlds. Gede Nibo is mischievous but also deeply powerful and wise. He is said to be able to see through the veil between life and death and uses his knowledge to help those seeking his guidance.

Legend tells of a young woman who was stricken with a serious illness. Her family called upon Gede Nibo for help, and he appeared to them as a skeleton carrying a cane and a top hat. He instructed the family to prepare a special offering of black coffee and rum and to place it at the crossroads. The family did as they were told, and he accepted their offering and healed the young woman, restoring her to full health.

Gede Nibo is also known for his love of music and dance and is often invoked during celebrations and festivals. One traditional dance that is associated with this spirit is the Banda dance, which involves a group of dancers moving in a circle while playing drums and other percussion instruments. In Haitian Vodou, Gede Nibo is often associated with the practice of ancestor veneration and is said to have the power to communicate with the spirits of the dead. Devotees may call upon Gede Nibo to help them connect with their ancestors and to seek their guidance and wisdom.

Preferred offerings for Gede Nibo include black coffee, rum, and cigars. Signs that he has received and accepted an offering may include the sudden appearance of a skeleton or a black dog or a sense of lightness and joy. Gede Nibo is celebrated and honored in New Orleans during the annual Vodou festival, Fet Gede, in late October or early November. During this festival, devotees offer gifts and perform rituals to honor Gede Nibo and the other Loa of death and the afterlife.

Gede Linto

This is a Lwa that is well known for making miracles happen. Like the rest of the Gede Lwa, he is all about death and fertility. Death isn't a bad thing when it comes to this family of Lwa, as it is simply a gateway to more life and part of the process of living. He is typically depicted as a dark man, about five feet tall, cane in hand, with glasses and an old-time black hat. It is said that he is one Gede Lwa who is particular about manners and is quite gentle. Some say he's a small, sweet boy known for his playful and mischievous nature and his love of candy and toys.

Gede Linto, when depicted as a young boy, is shown with curly hair and a playful smile. His veve, a symbol used in Vodou rituals to invoke the presence of a Loa, features a heart, a cross, and a lollipop. He is not syncretized with any saint in particular; still, he is considered a part of the Gede family of Loa, which is associated with death and the spirit world. He is said to be associated with the color pink and the herbs mint and cinnamon. He is known to have a particular fondness for candy and sweets, often offered to him during Vodou ceremonies. Linto's veve is like that of Lantor, with a cross with two circles on both sides and a heart beneath it.

Guede Masaka and Guede Oussou

Guede Masaka is associated with the color black. His veve often includes a skull, crossbones, and a heart. He is known for his ability to remove obstacles and provide protection. Guede Oussou is associated with purple, and his veve often includes a skull and crossbones with a snake. He is known for his association with the rainbow and is often called upon for his ability to bring good luck and prosperity. He is also known for his irreverent and mischievous nature and is often depicted as fond of alcohol and tobacco.

Guede Masaka and Guede Oussou are often referred to as "gravediggers" in Haitian Vodou. This is because they are believed to have the power to bury and exhume corpses. In Haitian Vodou, working with the dead is seen as a sacred and powerful skill, and both Guede are revered for their ability to navigate the realms of the dead. They are seen as powerful protectors and healers and are called upon for their ability to remove obstacles and provide spiritual guidance and support.

Guede Masaka and Guede Oussou are celebrated in Haitian Vodou during the annual Day of the Dead celebrations on November 1st and 2nd. During these celebrations, offerings of food, drink, and tobacco are made to the Guede, and they are honored and remembered as powerful and benevolent Lwa.

Gede Lantor

This Lwa is all about love and healing his devotees. What is interesting about him is that he is depicted as a woman with long, flowing hair. His correspondences include lightning and thunder, and he is known to assist anyone having issues with matters of the heart or sexuality. Lantor's veve looks like Linto's.

Chapter Six: The Petro Lwa

This chapter will discuss some of the most common Petro Lwa – so that you know everything there is to know about them! Knowing the Lwa will help you interact with them, make offerings, and more. It's easier to feel their presence in your life when you know who you're dealing with.

Simbi Andezo

Simbi Andezo is a water spirit in Haitian Vodou and New Orleans Voodoo. He is associated with the Simbi family of Loa; he is often depicted as a serpent, though he may also appear as a water snake or fish. He is known for his ability to grant knowledge, particularly of the secrets of the natural world, and for his healing powers.

His veve, or sacred symbol, typically includes a serpent or fish-like figure with a crescent moon and various other symbols representing water and knowledge. In Haitian Vodou, Simbi Andezo is often syncretized with Saint Patrick, while in New Orleans Voodoo, he may be associated with St. James the Greater or St. Dominic. His correspondences include blue and green and water-associated herbs such as basil, mint, and bay leaf.

Simbi Andezo has a close relationship with other members of the Simbi family of Loa and other water spirits, such as Agwe and La Sirene. In lore, he is often described as wise, knowledgeable, mischievous, and unpredictable. He enjoys offerings of rum, tobacco, and fish and may also appreciate gifts of knowledge, such as books or other educational materials. In Haitian Vodou, Simbi Andezo is celebrated on June 24th, the feast day of St. John the Baptist, also associated with water. In New

Orleans Voodoo, he may be honored on June 29th, the feast day of St. Peter, who is also associated with water. In Hoodoo, he may be called upon for his knowledge and healing powers through spells and charms.

Gran Bwa

Gran Bwa, the powerful Loa of the forest, is a force to be reckoned with in Haitian Vodou, New Orleans Voodoo, and Hoodoo. This ancient spirit has deep roots, and his influence is felt far and wide. In appearance, Gran Bwa is often depicted as a towering figure with a fierce and formidable presence. He is said to wear a hat made of leaves and be draped in foliage, symbolizing his deep connection to the natural world. His visage is often carved into totems and sculptures, and his image is used in veves, and other sacred symbols associated with his worship.

Regarding symbols, Gran Bwa's veve is a powerful image representing his essence and energy. It is a swirling, intricate pattern of lines and curves that is said to embody the spirit of the forest and the power of nature. His other associated symbols include trees, leaves, and various other flora and fauna found in the wilderness. While Gran Bwa is not syncretized with any particular saint, he is often associated with Saint Sebastian, a Christian martyr known for his deep devotion and unwavering faith. It is said that Gran Bwa shares many of these qualities and is a protector of the faithful.

Gran Bwa's correspondences include the colors green and brown, which are associated with the natural world and the forest. His preferred herbs and plants include basil, patchouli, and cedar, which have strong protective and purifying properties. His associations with the forest mean he is also closely linked to the animals that inhabit it, including the serpent, the owl, and the bear. Regarding his relationships with other Loa, Gran Bwa is known to be a solitary figure and often seen as a guardian or protector of the other spirits. His fierce and protective nature means that the other Loa deeply respect him, and his powers are often called upon during times of danger or strife.

Lore connected to Gran Bwa depicts him as a powerful and sometimes unpredictable force that must be treated with great respect and reverence. He is said to be wise and knowledgeable but also capable of great anger and retribution if his boundaries are crossed, or his sacred spaces are violated. Despite his fearsome reputation, however, he is also known to be a kind and caring protector, particularly of children and those who are vulnerable. Offerings to Gran Bwa often include offerings of food, drink, sacred herbs, and plants. He is particularly fond of rum, and offerings of this potent spirit are said to be especially pleasing. Signs that he has received and accepted an offering can include a sudden gust of wind, the rustling of leaves, or the appearance of an animal or bird associated with the forest.

In Haitian Vodou, New Orleans Voodoo, and Hoodoo, Gran Bwa is celebrated and honored in various ways. Offerings are made at altars dedicated to him, and his veve is drawn on the ground to summon his power and presence. Special ceremonies are also held in his honor, particularly during the Feast of Saint Sebastian, associated with his worship.

Ti Jean Petro

Ti Jean Petro is a powerful Loa in Haitian Vodou, known for his trickster nature, fierce energy, and connection to fire. Like many Loas, his appearance and personality can vary depending on the context and the worshiper's relationship with him. In some depictions, he is said to be a short, muscular man with a wild mane of hair, often wearing a red scarf or bandanna around his head. He is sometimes shown carrying a machete, a symbol of his warrior spirit, and may also be depicted with a serpent or a black rooster, both associated with his energy and power. The veve of Ti-Jean Petro is a complex and ornate design, featuring interlocking circles and a central image of a human figure with outstretched arms. Other associated symbols include the sun, a rooster, and red and black, representing his fiery and passionate nature. He is often syncretized with St. James the Greater, a Christian saint associated with war and battle. This connection highlights his fierce and protective energy and his ability to provide strength and courage to his followers.

Regarding correspondence, Ti Jean Petro is associated with the color red and plants and herbs such as hot peppers, ginger, and tobacco. His energy is said to be connected to fire and heat, and he is often called upon to provide protection, strength, and power in difficult situations. This spirit is closely connected with other Loas in the Vodou pantheon, particularly those associated with the Petro tradition, emphasizing fiery and aggressive energy. He is often associated with other powerful and intense Loas, such as Ezili Dantor, Papa Legba, and Baron Samedi, with whom he shares a connection to death and the underworld.

Lore surrounding Ti Jean Petro often emphasizes his trickster nature and his ability to outwit and manipulate others. He is said to enjoy playing pranks and tricks but also has a deeply compassionate and protective side, particularly for vulnerable or oppressed people. Offerings to this spirit may include red candles, spicy foods, and alcohol, as well as items such as knives, machetes, or other tools associated with his warrior energy. Signs that he has accepted an offering may include a feeling of heat or intense energy and sightings of roosters or other symbols associated with his energy. Ti Jean Petro is celebrated and honored in various ways throughout the Vodou tradition, particularly in the Petro tradition. His feast day is July 25th, typically marked by feasting, dancing, and other celebrations in his honor. In New Orleans Voodoo and Hoodoo, Ti Jean Petro is sometimes called "Papa Jean." He is often associated with the color red and with fiery, protective energy. He may be invoked in spells and rituals related to courage, strength, and overcoming obstacles.

Carrefour

Carrefour is a powerful and enigmatic Loa in Haitian Vodou, New Orleans Voodoo, and Hoodoo traditions. He is associated with crossroads, transitions, and change and is often called upon to bring luck, protection, and guidance. Depicted as a tall, thin man with dark skin, dressed in ragged clothes and carrying a cane, Carrefour is sometimes shown with a skull on his hat or necklace, symbolizing death and the crossing between worlds. His veve, or ritual symbol, is a complex pattern of interlocking triangles and circles, representing the intersections of paths and the power of change.

In Haitian Vodou, Carrefour is often syncretized with Saint Peter, the Christian apostle, and keeper of the keys to heaven. This connection reflects his role as a guardian of gateways and thresholds, both physical and spiritual. In New Orleans Voodoo, he is sometimes associated with Papa Legba, another Loa associated with crossroads and gatekeeping. His correspondences include black and red, representing death and life, respectively. His associated plants include horehound, tobacco, and cypress; his offerings may include rum, cigars, and chicken. He is also known to enjoy hot peppers and spicy foods, which represent his fiery nature.

In Haitian Vodou, Carrefour is often considered a powerful and feared Loa, associated with danger and chaos. He is known to be a trickster and a master of illusion and is said to be able to grant both blessings and curses. Despite this reputation, however, he is revered for his ability to bring about change and transformation and is sometimes called upon to help with legal or financial matters. In New Orleans Voodoo and Hoodoo, Carrefour is sometimes known as Papa La Bas and is associated with the city's historic Congo Square, a gathering place for enslaved Africans and their descendants. In these traditions, he is often called upon to protect the community and provide guidance during times of change and upheaval.

To honor and work with Carrefour, practitioners may create a sacred space with his veve and offer him appropriate offerings, such as rum, tobacco, or spicy foods. Signs that he has received and accepted an offering may include the appearance of black or red birds or the scent of cigar smoke. Carrefour is celebrated and honored in various ways throughout the year, including on January 6th, the feast day of Saint Peter, and during the Haitian Vodou festivals of Fet Gede and Fet Nago. In New Orleans Voodoo and Hoodoo traditions, he may be honored during Mardi Gras and other celebrations that emphasize crossing boundaries and the transformation of the self.

Ezili Gé Rouge

Ezili Gé Rouge, the "Red-Eyed Lady," is a powerful and complex Lwa in Haitian Vodou. She is often associated with love, beauty, passion, and sensuality but also with war, fire, and destruction. In her visual representation, this Lwa is often depicted as a beautiful woman with piercing red eyes dressed in red and black clothing. She may wear a crown of thorns or have a snake wrapped around her neck. Her veve, or sacred symbol, features a heart with an arrow through it, surrounded by flames. While she is not syncretized with a Catholic saint, some practitioners may associate her with Saint Barbara or Saint Catherine.

Ezili Gé Rouge's correspondences include the colors red and black, the herbs vervain and dragon's blood, and the flowers hibiscus and red roses. She is associated with fire, lightning, and the element of air. She may be invoked alongside other Ezili spirits like Ezili Dantor and Ezili Freda. She is also said to have connections to the Lwa Ogou and Agwe. Lore surrounding Ezili Gé Rouge often depicts her as a powerful and passionate figure, quick to anger but also fiercely protective of her devotees. She is seen as a force to be reckoned with, capable of great love and destruction.

Offerings to this Lwa may include red wine, red candles, spicy foods, and perfume. Devotees may also offer her blood, which is not recommended for inexperienced practitioners. Signs that she has received and accepted an offering may include strong winds, sudden flames, or the scent of burning roses. Ezili Gé Rouge is honored in Haitian Vodou through private and public ceremonies, often held on Fridays. Although practices may differ, she may also be celebrated in New Orleans Voodoo and Hoodoo traditions. Her devotees may dance, sing, and offer offerings in her honor, seeking her protection, guidance, and blessings in matters of love, relationships, and passion.

Ezili Dantor

Ezili Dantor, the Haitian Vodou goddess of love, motherhood, and protection, is a powerful and revered figure in the pantheon of Loa. Her image is that of a fierce and protective mother, often depicted with a child in her arms, a machete in one hand, and a fiery torch in the other. She is known to be both nurturing and fiercely protective, fiercely loyal to her children, and unafraid to defend them against any threat. Her veve is a depiction of a heart pierced by a sword, surrounded by the letters of her name. She is syncretized with the Catholic figure of the Black Madonna, and her colors are typically red and blue. Her correspondences include the herbs basil, rue, vervain, and the plants rose and hibiscus. She is associated with the number 9; her favorite foods are pork, eggplant, and bread.

Ezili Dantor is known to have close relationships with other Loa, including Ogou, the god of war, and Erzili Freda, the goddess of love and beauty. She is often seen as a protector of women and children and is also associated with lesbianism and same-sex relationships. According to lore, she is a fierce and protective mother figure who will go to great lengths to defend her children. One story tells of her using her machete to cut off her head and offer it to the spirit of her daughter, who had been captured and enslaved by white plantation owners.

Preferred offerings to Ezili Dantor include red and blue candles, flowers, and sweet-smelling oils. Signs that she has received and accepted an offering can include the smell of sweet perfume or flowers and a feeling of warmth or comfort. Ezili Dantor is celebrated and honored in Haitian Vodou, New Orleans Voodoo, and Hoodoo. In Haitian Vodou, she is often associated with the Petwo rites, known for their intense and fiery energy. Her feast day is celebrated on May 30th, and offerings are made at her altars in hopes of gaining her protection and blessings.

In New Orleans Voodoo and Hoodoo, she is often associated with the figure of Marie Laveau, the famous Voodoo queen who was said to have worshipped Ezili Dantor. Her image can be found in many Voodoo and Hoodoo shops, and offerings are made to her in hopes of gaining her assistance in matters of love, protection, and fertility. In all of her incarnations, Ezili Dantor is a powerful and revered figure known for her fierce love and unwavering protection. She is a symbol of strength and resilience and a reminder that even in the face of great adversity, we can find the courage and fortitude to overcome.

Agwe La Flambeau

Agwe La Flambeau is a powerful and respected Loa in Haitian Vodou, New Orleans Voodoo, and Hoodoo traditions. He is the spirit of the sea and is associated with water, the ocean, and all aquatic life. This Lwa is often depicted as a strong and muscular man with skin as dark as the ocean depths. He wears a long blue coat and a captain's hat, symbolizing his command over the vast expanse of the sea. His veve is a complex symbol that incorporates a variety of marine life, including fish, seashells, and waves. It is often drawn in white or blue powder and is used in ceremonies to call upon his energy and power. Other symbols associated with Agwe include boats, anchors, and tridents.

In some syncretic traditions, Agwe is associated with Saint Ulrich, who is revered in some areas of Haiti as the patron saint of seafarers. However, he is not syncretized to any particular saint in other traditions. He is associated with the color blue, representing the ocean and the depths of the sea. His sacred plants include seaweed, sea grape, and sea lavender. Offerings to him often include seafood, such as fish, crab, or lobster, as well as blue candles and blue flowers.

Agwe is closely associated with other water spirits like La Sirène and Simbi. He is also believed to work closely with the Gede, the spirits of the dead, in ceremonies taking place on the water. All the tales about this Lwa depict him as a powerful and benevolent spirit who is fiercely protective of those who call upon him. He is known to calm even the roughest of seas and provide safe passage for those who travel on the water. In some stories, Agwe is also associated with wealth and prosperity, as he is believed to control the ocean's vast resources. Signs that he has accepted an offering may include an increase in the strength of the ocean currents or the appearance of dolphins or other marine life near a boat. Offerings may also be marked by the appearance of a blue flame, which is believed to be a sign of his presence.

Agwe is celebrated and honored in various ceremonies and rituals in Haitian Vodou, New Orleans Voodoo, and Hoodoo. In some traditions, he is honored on the feast day of Saint Ulrich, while in others, he has his own dedicated ceremonies. Many ceremonies dedicated to this spirit take place on the water, with offerings made to him at the sea's edge or on boats sent out into the open ocean. These ceremonies often involve music, dance, and drumming to call upon Agwe's power and honor his role as the spirit of the sea.

Ogun Petro

Ogun Petro is a powerful and dynamic Loa in Haitian Vodou, with a fiery personality and a strong presence that commands respect. He is associated with fire, iron, and metalworking and is often depicted as a blacksmith, wielding his hammer and anvil with strength and skill. In his human form, this Lwa is often described as tall and muscular, with dark skin and piercing eyes that seem to glow with the intensity of the flames he commands. He wears a red or black hat and a red or white scarf around his neck, sometimes adorned with a necklace of iron or other metals. The veve of Ogun Petro is a complex and powerful symbol, often featuring a central image of a hammer and anvil, surrounded by fiery symbols and other motifs associated with metalworking and the forge. It is said that his veve has the power to open doorways and summon his spirit, so it is treated with great reverence and respect by practitioners of Haitian Vodou.

Ogun Petro is syncretized with the Catholic saint, St. James the Greater, who is often depicted as a warrior or a pilgrim, wielding a sword and wearing a hat adorned with scallop shells. This association with St. James reflects Lwa's reputation as a powerful and fierce protector of his followers, who will stop at nothing to defend them from harm and injustice. In terms of his correspondences, Ogun Petro is associated with the color red and iron, steel, and other metals. He is also associated with herbs and plants such as basil, rue, and tobacco, which are often used in offerings and rituals dedicated to him.

Ogun is known for his close relationships with other powerful Loa, including Ezili Dantor, Baron Samedi, and Papa Legba. He is particularly close to the fiery Loa known as Met Kalfou, with whom he shares a powerful bond based on their shared association with fire and the forge. This iron Lwa is often depicted as a fierce and unyielding warrior, willing to take on any challenge or foe to protect his people. He is often associated with acts of bravery and heroism and is seen as a symbol of strength, determination, and courage in the face of adversity.

Preferred offerings to Ogun Petro include offerings of meat, rum, and other strong spirits, as well as metal objects such as knives, tools, or even automobile parts. Signs that he has received and accepted one's offerings may include the flickering of flames or the sound of metal clanging in the distance. Ogun Petro is often honored through fiery ceremonies involving bonfires, sparks, and the pounding of metal. These celebrations may occur at specific times of the year, such as the Feast of St. James in July, or they may be held in honor of specific events or occasions. In New Orleans Voodoo and Hoodoo, Ogun Petro is often associated with the powerful ritual of "cutting and clearing," which involves using metal tools to clear away negative energy and obstacles in one's life.

Chapter Seven: Voodoo and Hoodoo Altars

Do You Need a Shrine or an Altar?

In the practice of Voodoo and Hoodoo, an altar or shrine can be a powerful tool used to connect with the spiritual world. It serves as a focal point for your devotion, gives a space for your offerings, and is a dedicated place for your prayers. But the question remains. Is an altar or shrine necessary?

A voodoo shrine.[11]

The answer to this question is both yes and no. It ultimately depends on your personal beliefs and practices. For some, an altar is an essential part of their spiritual practice. For others, it is not necessary. Suppose you find comfort and connection in having a physical space for your spiritual practice. In that case, an altar can be a powerful tool. You can use your altar to honor your ancestors, deities, or saints. You can also use it to create a space for your prayers, to offer thanks, or to seek guidance.

The act of setting up an altar can be a meditative and intentional process. You can choose items that have personal significance to you, such as candles, crystals, statues, or pictures. You can also use items that are traditionally associated with Voodoo and Hoodoo, such as graveyard dirt, red brick dust, or mojo bags. Your altar can be as simple or elaborate as you like. It can be a small corner of your room or an entire room dedicated to your practice. The key is to create a space that feels sacred to you, a space that allows you to connect with the spiritual world in a meaningful way.

But what if you are someone who does not feel the need for an altar or shrine or who, for some reason, cannot set one up? Is it still possible to connect with the spiritual world without one? The answer is yes. You do not need a physical space to connect with the spiritual world. You can connect with the divine through your thoughts, actions, and intentions. You can offer prayers and thanks wherever you are, whether you are in a crowded city or a quiet forest. Do not feel discouraged if you do not have the space or resources to create an altar. There are many ways to connect with the spiritual world without one. You can create a virtual altar using images and symbols that resonate with you. You can also simply take a moment each day to reflect on your spirituality, offer thanks, or ask for guidance.

Ultimately, whether or not you choose to have an altar or shrine is a personal decision. It is important to honor your beliefs and practices and create a spiritual practice that *feels authentic.* Whether you create a physical space for your practice or connect with the spiritual world in other ways, know that your intentions and devotion truly matter. In Voodoo and Hoodoo, the most important aspect of your practice is your connection to the spiritual world. Whether you choose to have an altar or not, the key is approaching your practice with reverence and respect. The spiritual world is a powerful and sacred place, and it is up to you to create a practice that honors its complexity and beauty.

If you choose to create an altar or shrine, there are several considerations to remember. First, choosing a location that feels sacred to you is important. This may be a corner of your room, a dedicated space in your home, or even a space outside. The key is to choose a location that feels comfortable and conducive to your spiritual practice. Second, choosing items that are personally significant to you is important. This may include candles, crystals, statues, or pictures. You may also choose items traditionally associated with Voodoo and Hoodoo, such as graveyard dirt, red brick dust, or mojo bags. The items you choose should be meaningful to you and help you connect with the spiritual world personally and authentically.

Third, it is important to set intentions for your altar or shrine. What do you hope to achieve through your practice? With whom do you hope to connect? Setting intentions allows you to create a focused and intentional practice that helps you achieve your spiritual goals. Finally, it is important to maintain your altar or shrine with care and respect. Keep it clean and organized, and refresh your offerings regularly. Take time each day to connect with your altar and to offer your prayers and thanks.

How to Create a Voodoo Altar for a Lwa

Creating a Voodoo altar dedicated to a specific Lwa can be a powerful and transformative experience. An altar can serve as a physical space for you to connect with the spiritual world and deepen your relationship with a specific Lwa. In this guide, you'll get some useful ideas on creating a Voodoo altar dedicated to a specific Lwa and some tips on how to honor and connect with your chosen Lwa.

Step One – Choosing your Lwa: First, choosing a Lwa to which you feel a strong connection is important. The Lwa are spirits that serve as intermediaries between the human and divine worlds. Each Lwa has its own personality, energy, and areas of influence. Some of the most well-known Lwa include Papa Legba, Baron Samedi, Ezili Danto, and Ogun. Research and explore the different Lwa to find one that resonates with you.

Step Two – Choosing and cleansing the space: Once you have chosen a Lwa, it is time to create your altar. Find a space in your home that feels sacred, and that can be dedicated to your practice. You can use a small table, a shelf, or even a corner of your room. Cleanse the space with some sage or incense to clear any negative energy and create a sacred atmosphere.

Step Three — Choosing what goes on your altar: Next, choose some items associated with your chosen Lwa to place on your altar. These may include candles, herbs, crystals, statues, or other symbolic items. For example, suppose you are creating an altar for Papa Legba. In that case, you may choose to place a statue of him on your altar, along with a white candle, some tobacco, and some rum. Suppose you are creating an altar for Ezili Danto. In that case, you may choose to place a statue of her on your altar, along with some red candles, some roses, and some champagne.

When placing your items on the altar, consider the energy and symbolism of each item. Each item should have a specific purpose and intention. For example, candles can represent the light and energy of the divine, while herbs can be used for protection and healing. Choose items that feel meaningful to you and that help you connect with the energy of your chosen Lwa.

Step Four — Connecting with your Lwa: Once you have set up your altar, it is time to connect with your chosen Lwa. One way to do this is through prayer and offerings. Light a candle and some incense, and offer some food or drink to your Lwa. Speak to your Lwa from your heart, and ask for their guidance and protection. You may also choose to perform a ritual or a dance to honor your Lwa and deepen your connection.

Another way to connect with your chosen Lwa is through meditation and visualization. Sit in front of your altar and close your eyes. Visualize your chosen Lwa standing in front of you, and imagine yourself surrounded by their energy and protection. Allow yourself to be open to any messages or guidance your Lwa may offer.

Step Five — Caring for your altar: Maintaining your altar with care and respect is important. Keep it clean and organized, and refresh your offerings regularly. Take time each day to connect with your altar and to offer your prayers and thanks.

Switching Your Voodoo Altar to a Hoodoo One

Changing your Voodoo altar to a Hoodoo one can be a meaningful transformation in your spiritual practice. Hoodoo is a form of African American folk magic closely related to Voodoo but has unique traditions and practices. If you are interested in incorporating Hoodoo into your practice, you can do a few things to change your Voodoo altar to a

Hoodoo one.

First, it is important to understand the differences between Voodoo and Hoodoo. While both traditions share some commonalities, Hoodoo is often more focused on practical magic and spellwork, while Voodoo focuses more on spiritual connection and ritual. Hoodoo also emphasizes the use of herbs, roots, and other natural materials in spellwork.

To change your Voodoo altar to a Hoodoo one, add some Hoodoo-specific items to your altar. These may include herbs, roots, oils, and other ingredients commonly used in Hoodoo spells. You can also add some symbolic items, such as a mojo bag or a small mirror, often used in Hoodoo magic.

Another way to change your Voodoo altar to a Hoodoo one is to incorporate some specific Hoodoo rituals and practices into your daily routine. For example, you can perform a daily spiritual bath or use a specific oil to anoint yourself before spellwork. You can also incorporate some specific prayers or chants associated with Hoodoo.

Setting Up Your Altar for Ancestral Veneration

If you are interested in ancestral veneration, you can also change your altar to make it suitable for this practice. Ancestral veneration is the practice of honoring and connecting with your ancestors, who are seen as powerful spiritual guides and protectors. Here are some helpful tips for creating an ancestral veneration altar:

Incorporate their photos: Incorporating photos or portraits of your ancestors on your altar can be a powerful way to visually connect with them during your worship. When you place a photo of your ancestor or ancestors on your altar, it serves as a reminder of their presence in your life and their relevance to your family history. It can be a way to honor their memory and acknowledge their contributions to your life and the lives of your ancestors. Photos of your ancestors on your altar can also help create a sacred space for you to connect with them. When you sit down to worship at your altar, seeing the faces of your ancestors can create a sense of comfort and familiarity. It can help you to feel less alone and more connected to your family history and ancestry.

Furthermore, incorporating photos of your ancestors can be a way to keep their memory alive. As time passes, it can be easy to forget the details of your family history and your ancestors' stories. However, by displaying their photos on your altar, you keep their memory alive and preserve their legacy for future generations. When choosing which photos to display on your altar, you may want to consider selecting images that are meaningful to you or represent significant moments in your family's history. For example, you may choose a photo of your great-grandmother on her wedding day or a photo of your grandfather during his military service. You may also choose to display photos of ancestors who have passed away more recently to honor their memory and keep their spirits close.

Additionally, it is important to treat the photos of your ancestors with respect and care. You may want to consider framing or placing them in protective sleeves to prevent damage or deterioration over time. You may also want to periodically clean the photos or arrange them in a way that feels aesthetically pleasing to you.

Use the items that they once owned: These items could be anything with personal significance or sentimental value, such as jewelry, clothing, or other heirlooms. Placing these items on your altar creates a tangible connection to your family history and ancestors. When you see and touch these items, you can connect with your ancestors in a more visceral way. It can be a powerful experience to hold something your ancestor once owned or wore and feel you are a part of their legacy.

Placing these items on your altar can also serve as a way to honor the memory of your ancestors and respect their contributions to your family history. For example, you may display a piece of jewelry passed down through several generations of your family or a garment your great-grandmother hand-sewed. These items can remind you of the sacrifices and hard work that your ancestors put into building your family legacy. When placing these items on your altar, it is important to treat them carefully. You could consider placing them on a special cloth or display stand or arranging them in a way that feels aesthetically pleasing to you. You may also want to clean the items periodically to prevent damage or deterioration.

Offer them their favorite food and drink: This can be a powerful way to honor their memory and create a sense of connection with them through shared experiences and traditions. Offering food or drink to your ancestors can be done in various ways. One approach is to offer something significant to them during their life. For example, suppose your grandmother loved a particular type of tea. In that case, you could offer that tea on your altar as a way to connect with her and honor her memory. Similarly, if your grandfather had a favorite food or drink, you could consider offering that item on your altar in his honor.

Another approach is to prepare a special dish or beverage aimed specifically at your ancestors' memory. This could be a family recipe passed down through the generations or a dish you create based on your ancestors' cultural traditions. By preparing this food or drink and offering it on your altar, you are creating a sense of continuity with your family history and honoring the traditions and customs of your ancestors. When offering food or drink on your altar, it is important to do so with care and respect. You might choose to place the food or drink on a special plate or cup or arrange it in a way that feels aesthetically pleasing to you. You may also want to light candles or incense to further honor your ancestors and create a sacred space for their memory.

Frequently Asked Questions

Q: Is it okay to have multiple altars?

A: Yes, it is absolutely okay to have multiple altars. In fact, many practitioners have separate altars for different purposes, such as one for ancestors, one for Lwas, and one for other spiritual beings. Having multiple altars allows you to focus your energy on specific practice areas. It can help you create a more personalized and meaningful spiritual practice.

Q: If I dedicate an altar to both an ancestor and a Lwa, would that be fine?

A: It is perfectly fine to dedicate an altar to an ancestor and a Lwa. In Voodoo, ancestors and Lwas are often seen as interconnected, and it is not uncommon for practitioners to honor both on the same altar. Just follow any specific rituals or practices associated with each spirit and show them both the respect they deserve.

Q: May I dedicate my altar to several Lwas?

A: Yes, it is possible to dedicate your altar to multiple Lwas, although it is important to do so with care and respect. Before dedicating your altar to multiple Lwas, make sure that you understand each Lwa's characteristics and requirements and that you can provide the necessary offerings and attention to each spirit. For instance, you should never have the same altar for a Rada and a Petro Lwa unless you've partitioned the altar so that one half is dedicated to each nanchon.

Q: What should I do with the food offerings after a while?

A: It is important to dispose of food offerings respectfully. In many Voodoo traditions, it is common to leave offerings out for a certain period (such as 24 hours) and then dispose of them naturally, such as burying them in the earth or throwing them into running water. Be sure to do so in a way that is respectful to the spirits and to the environment.

Q: How do I cleanse the altar?

A: Cleansing the altar is important to maintaining a spiritual practice. Depending on your specific tradition and preferences, there are many ways to cleanse an altar. One common method is to use smoke from herbs or incense, such as sage or palo santo. You can also use sounds like a bell or a singing bowl to clear negative energy. Another approach is to physically clean the altar with water and mild soap while focusing on the intention of cleansing and purifying the space. Whatever method you choose, be sure to do so with care and intention, and always show respect for the spirits and the altar itself.

Q: Can I use my altar for divination or spellwork?

A: Altars can be used for various spiritual practices, including divination and spellwork. However, it is important to approach these practices with care and respect and to follow any specific rituals or traditions associated with them. If you are new to divination or spellwork, it would be helpful to seek guidance from a more experienced practitioner or to extensively research and practice before attempting these spiritual practices on your own.

Q: How often should I clean and refresh my altar?

A: The frequency with which you clean and refresh your altar will depend on your specific practice and the spirits with which you are working. Some practitioners prefer to clean their altar daily or weekly, while others may only do so on special occasions or when working with specific spirits. It is important to listen to your intuition and the guidance of the spirits when it comes to maintaining your altar. You should always show respect and care for the space used and the spirits you are working with.

Q: What should I do if my altar is disturbed or damaged?

A: If your altar is disturbed or damaged in any way, it is important to take the necessary steps to restore it as soon as possible. The first thing you should do is assess the extent of the damage. If it is minor, you may be able to repair it yourself. You may need to consult a spiritual practitioner or elder for guidance if it is more extensive. Regardless of the extent of the damage, it is important to cleanse and re-consecrate the altar after it has been repaired. This can be done by smudging the area with sage or palo santo, anointing the altar with holy water or Florida water, and offering prayers and offerings to the spirits to ask for their forgiveness and blessings. It is also important to investigate the cause of the disturbance or damage. If it was due to natural causes such as a storm or earthquake, you might need to perform a special ritual to appease the spirits of the land. If it was due to human interference, you might need to perform a more involved ritual to remove any negative energy and protect your altar from future harm.

Chapter Eight: Mojo Bags and Gris-Gris

Mojo bags and gris-gris are among the most important Voodoo charms, even though most people seem to know only about Voodoo dolls which are actually a form of gris-gris on their own. In this chapter, you'll learn everything about these charms and their uses, as well as how to make them.

A mojo bag.[12]

Gris-Gris? Mojo Bags?

Mojo bags and gris-gris are powerful charms rooted in Voodoo beliefs and practices. These objects are more than mere trinkets. They are imbued with spiritual power and meaning and are integral to the Voodoo tradition. Sometimes they're known as monjo or jomo bags. Mojo bags are small, usually flannel or leather pouches filled with herbs, roots, stones, and other magical ingredients. They are often carried on by the person or can be placed in a specific location, such as on an altar or in a sacred space.

Gris-gris, on the other hand, is more specific to the New Orleans Voodoo tradition. The word "gris-gris" is believed to come from the Yoruba word for juju. Some say it's from the French word "*joujou,*" which refers to a plaything or toy. Gris-gris are also bags filled with magical ingredients, but they are usually worn on a string around the neck or waist. Gris-gris can also be used in other forms, such as small cloth dolls, totems, or even powders.

Both mojo bags and gris-gris are deeply connected to Voodoo beliefs and practices. In the Voodoo tradition, everything in the universe is believed to be imbued with spiritual energy. This energy can be harnessed and used for various purposes, from healing to protection to love spells. Mojo bags and gris-gris are tools that Voodoo practitioners use to access this energy and channel it toward a specific goal. In Voodoo, the ingredients that go into mojo bags and gris-gris are carefully chosen for their spiritual properties. For example, herbs like basil, rosemary, and mint are believed to have protective qualities, while roots like mandrake, sarsaparilla, and ginseng are thought to have healing powers. Stones like amethyst, quartz, and hematite are believed to have different energies, used for different purposes.

How mojo bags and gris-gris are made and used also reflects Voodoo beliefs and practices. These charms are often made during specific phases of the moon or during certain times of the year when the spiritual energy is believed to be particularly strong. The person making the charm may also perform specific rituals or prayers to imbue it with additional power. The uses of mojo bags and gris-gris are as varied as the ingredients that go into them. They can be used for protection, luck, love, money, and even to curse an enemy. In some cases, they may be combined with other Voodoo practices, such as candle magic or spiritual baths.

In Voodoo, mojo bags and gris-gris are considered to be very personal objects. They are often made specifically for an individual and may even contain personal items like hair or fingernail clippings. It is believed that the closer the connection between the individual and the charm, the more powerful it will be.

How to Make Your Mojo Bag

Creating a mojo bag is a sacred ritual that requires care and attention. Before beginning, choosing the right materials and setting your intentions is important. A mojo bag is a personal item; each should be crafted with love and care. To make a mojo bag, you will need the following materials:

- A small piece of cloth or bag made from natural materials (such as cotton, silk, or leather)
- Herbs, roots, or other natural ingredients (such as bones, crystals, or coins) which correspond to your intention
- Thread or string
- Scissors
- Anointing oil (optional)

Now that you have gathered your materials, it is time to begin:

1. **Set your intention:** Before you start, it's important to set your intention. Decide what you want your mojo bag to do for you. For example, do you want it to bring you love, success, or protection? This intention will guide your selection of materials.
2. **Choose your ingredients:** Select herbs, roots, or other natural items which correspond with your intention. Consider consulting the plant and herb symbolism guide in the previous chapter of this book for guidance.
3. **Cut the cloth:** Cut a small square of cloth, or use a pre-made bag large enough to hold your ingredients.
4. **Add your ingredients**: Place your chosen ingredients inside the bag or on the cloth. *Be careful to choose only those items which correspond to your intention.* For example, if you want to attract love, you may use rose petals, cinnamon, and catnip. If you want protection, you could use a piece of hematite, sage, and a pinch of salt.

5. **Tie the bag:** After adding ingredients, carefully tie up the bag or cloth using the string or thread. As you tie the bag, focus on your intention, and ask for the blessings of the spirits and ancestors.
6. **Anoint the bag (optional):** You can anoint your bag with an oil corresponding to your intention. For example, if you want to attract love, you could use rose oil. You could use a protective oil such as frankincense if you want protection.
7. **Personalize the bag:** Your mojo bag should be a personal item that reflects your individual spirit. You can personalize it by adding a small talisman or charm representing you or something important to you. This could be a piece of jewelry or a small trinket.
8. **Consecrate the bag:** You should consecrate your mojo bag by placing it on your altar and asking for the blessings of the spirits and ancestors. You can also cleanse it in the smoke of burned incense or sage to eliminate any negative energy.
9. **Breathe on the bag:** Exhale through your mouth thrice onto the bag. This will activate it so it can get to work on the intention you set for it.

By following these steps, you can create a powerful and effective mojo bag imbued with the energy of your intentions and the blessings of your spirits and ancestors. Remember to treat your mojo bag with respect and care, and always keep it close to you for maximum effectiveness.

How to Make Your Gris-Gris

Making a gris-gris is a sacred and deeply personal practice in Voodoo. It involves choosing materials with specific meanings and intentions and creating a unique charm representing your desires and needs. To begin, gather the following materials:

- A piece of fabric, preferably red or black
- Needle and thread
- Herbs and spices, such as basil, cinnamon, or mint
- Small crystals or stones, such as clear quartz or black tourmaline
- Personal items, such as hair or nail clippings
- Paper and pen

A charm or talisman, such as a small piece of jewelry or a coin Once you have gathered your materials, follow these steps to create your gris-gris:

1. **Choose your intention**: Before you begin, it is important to know what you want to achieve with your gris-gris. Take some time to reflect on your desires and write them down on a piece of paper.
2. **Choose your materials**: Each herb, crystal, and personal item has its own meaning and energy. Choose items that align with your intention and add them to your work area.
3. **Cut your fabric:** Cut a small piece of fabric into a square or rectangle. The size of the fabric will depend on the size of your charm.
4. **Write your intention:** Using a pen or marker, write your intention on a small piece of paper. Fold the paper and place it in the center of the fabric.
5. **Add your herbs and spices:** Sprinkle a small number of herbs and spices onto the fabric. Each herb and spice has its own meaning, so choose ones that align with your intention. Fold the fabric over and sew the edges together, creating a small pouch.
6. **Add your crystals and personal items:** Add your crystals and personal items to the pouch. These items will add personal energy to your gris-gris and help align it with your intention.
7. **Add your charm:** Choose a charm or talisman representing your intention and add it to the pouch. This could be a small piece of jewelry or a coin.
8. **Close your gris-gris:** Once you have added all of your materials, close your gris-gris by tying it with a piece of thread. You can also sew it closed if you prefer.
9. **Cleanse and charge your gris-gris:** Hold it in your hands and focus your intention on it. You can also cleanse and charge it by placing it in the moonlight or smudging it with sage or palo santo.
10. **Breathe on the gris-gris**: Doing this will set it to work on whatever you made it for.

Remember, creating a gris-gris is a personal and sacred practice. Choose materials that align with your intention and trust your intuition. Look at the glossary at the end of the book for more ideas on what sort of materials you could use, as well as their spiritual meanings, so you can get more creative with your craft. May your mojo bag and gris-gris bring you the blessings and protection you seek!

Uses of Voodoo Charms

Protection: Mojo bags and gris-gris can be used for protection from negative energies, bad luck, and harm. Regarding voodoo practices, protection is one of the most common uses for mojo bags and gris-gris. These voodoo charms are believed to provide spiritual and physical protection against negative energies, bad luck, and harm.

In voodoo, protection is not just about physical safety but also about spiritual well-being. It is believed that negative energies and influences can attach to a person, causing emotional and mental distress. Mojo bags and gris-gris are thought to protect against these negative energies and help the person use them to maintain a sense of spiritual and emotional balance.

Love and relationships: Voodoo charms can attract or enhance love and strengthen relationships. Voodoo charms can also be used to bring harmony into relationships and deepen the connection between partners. Love and relationship charms can be made using various ingredients and symbols believed to have properties associated with love, passion, and romance. Symbols can be used in love and relationship charms. For example, a charm can be made using two interlocking hearts to represent a couple's love for each other. One or both partners can carry the charm to strengthen the bond between them. Other symbols that can be used include Cupid's arrow, which represents the power of love and attraction, and the infinity symbol, which represents the everlasting nature of love.

Using love and relationship charms can help to bring more love and harmony into your life. By focusing your energy and intentions on attracting love or enhancing your relationship, you can create positive energy to draw more love and happiness into your life. It is important to remember that love charms are not a substitute for healthy communication and actions in relationships but rather a tool to support and enhance the love that already exists.

Health and healing: Mojo bags and gris-gris can be used for physical, emotional, and spiritual healing. They can be powerful tools to promote physical, emotional, and spiritual healing. These charms can help alleviate ailments and provide strength and protection during illness. The materials used in creating these charms can have healing properties, and the intention and energy infused into the charm can help amplify these properties.

When creating a mojo bag or gris-gris for healing purposes, it is important to set the intention for the charm and focus on the desired outcome. The materials used in the charm should be chosen based on their healing properties, and the charm should be infused with positive energy and intention. The charm can then be carried or worn to promote healing and protection. It is important to note that while mojo bags and gris-gris can be powerful tools for promoting healing, they should not replace medical treatment. It is always important to seek medical advice and treatment when dealing with health issues. Mojo bags and gris-gris can be used alongside medical treatment to promote healing and well-being.

Prosperity and abundance: In Voodoo, prosperity and abundance are considered important aspects of a well-lived life. While financial wealth is not the only measure of prosperity, it is certainly an important aspect of it. Voodoo charms can attract wealth, success, and abundance in all areas of life. The use of mojo bags and gris-gris in Voodoo is often linked to harnessing the universe's power to achieve one's goals. It is believed that by creating a physical representation of one's desires, such as a mojo bag or gris-gris, and imbuing it with spiritual power, you can draw the desired outcome into your life.

For those seeking prosperity and abundance, Voodoo charms can attract wealth and success and increase opportunities for financial gain. These charms may include symbolic items such as coins or dollar bills, herbs, and other natural materials believed to have magical properties. It is important to note that Voodoo does not teach that wealth and prosperity are the only measures of success or happiness. Rather, true prosperity is believed to encompass all aspects of life, including emotional, spiritual, and social well-being. Therefore, Voodoo charms used for prosperity and abundance may also include personal growth and fulfillment items, such as crystals or symbols of personal goals.

Overall, Voodoo charms used for prosperity and abundance are intended to help individuals align their energy with the universe, increasing the likelihood of success in all areas of life. While financial gain is often a desired outcome, true prosperity also involves emotional and spiritual fulfillment, making Voodoo a holistic approach to achieving prosperity and abundance.

Legal matters: Mojo bags and gris-gris are not just used for spiritual purposes but can also be used to aid in legal matters. These charms can help with success in court cases or negotiations, as well as giving protection from legal harm. The power of these charms lies in their ability to connect the individual to the spiritual realm and provide guidance and protection. Voodoo practitioners believe that by creating a mojo bag or gris-gris, they are tapping into the power of their ancestors and spirits to guide them in their legal matters.

These charms can be carried on your body or placed strategically to provide maximum benefit. When used in legal matters, the mojo bag or gris-gris can help to provide a clear mind and a strong presence, making it easier to present a strong case or negotiate favorable terms. In addition, the mojo bag or gris-gris can protect from negative energy, including those directed toward the individual in legal proceedings. This can help ensure the individual is not wrongfully accused or unfairly punished.

Spiritual connection: Voodoo charms attract material blessings or protection from negative energies and can also enhance your spiritual connections. The practice of Voodoo involves a belief in the existence of a spirit world that is interconnected with the physical world. Because of this, Voodoo charms can be used to enhance spiritual connections with the divine, ancestors, and spirits. One way voodoo charms can help with spiritual connection is by physically representing your intentions and prayers. When you create a mojo bag or gris-gris, you physically manifest your desires and needs. By carrying or wearing the charm, you remind yourself of your spiritual goals and the energy you put into achieving them.

In addition, voodoo charms can be used in rituals or ceremonies to enhance spiritual connections. For example, a mojo bag may be used in a ritual to connect with ancestors or ask spirits for guidance. The presence of the charm can serve as a focal point for your intentions and prayers, allowing you to deepen your spiritual connections. Furthermore, the materials used to create voodoo charms can also have spiritual significance. For example, certain herbs or crystals are believed to have spiritual properties that can enhance spiritual connections or help in spiritual healing. By including these materials in a mojo bag or gris-gris, you are utilizing their spiritual properties to enhance your own spiritual connections.

Tips and Tricks to Adapt Charms to Your Needs

1. **Personalize the ingredients:** While traditional ingredients are often used in mojo bags and gris-gris, choosing ingredients that resonate with you and your intentions is important. Consider using herbs or other materials with personal significance or specific properties that align with your desired outcome.

2. **Customize the color:** The color of the fabric used to make a mojo bag or gris-gris can also be personalized to fit your intentions. Consider choosing a color corresponding to the specific purpose of your charm, such as green for money or red for love.

3. **Incorporate personal items:** Adding personal items to your mojo bag or gris-gris can help strengthen your connection to the charm and your intentions. This could include a piece of jewelry, a small photo, or a written intention.

4. **Charge and activate the charm:** Before using your charm, take the time to charge it with your intentions and activate its energy. This can be done through prayer, meditation, or other ritual practices. *Remember that breathing on the charm is vital.*

5. **Recharge the charm as needed:** As you continue to use your mojo bag or gris-gris, it may lose some of its energy over time. Consider recharging it periodically with intention-setting and energy-activating practices to keep it effective.

Chapter Nine: Cleansing and Raising Protections

While the popular media often portrays Voodoo and Hoodoo as being all about curses and hexes, the truth is that the best offense is a good defense. It's essential to remember that Voodoo and Hoodoo are primarily spiritual practices that focus on protection, healing, and helping people achieve their goals. One of the most effective ways to protect yourself is by taking a spiritual bath. This practice involves using a combination of herbs, oils, and other ingredients to cleanse yourself spiritually and protect yourself from negative energies. When done correctly, a spiritual bath can help you feel more balanced, centered, and grounded, as well as help you release any negative energy you may be carrying around.

In addition to spiritual baths, there are various rituals and spells you can use to protect yourself from negative energies and influences. These could include creating a protective charm or talisman, performing a ritual to banish negative energy, or casting a spell to protect yourself from harm. Another important aspect of protection in Voodoo and Hoodoo is working with spiritual allies. This could include calling on your ancestors or other spirits for protection and guidance or creating a relationship with a particular deity or spirit who is known for providing protection and support.

There are a number of rituals and spells available that provide protection.[18]

One of the most important things to remember when working with protection in Voodoo and Hoodoo is that it's not just about defending yourself from outside influences. It's also about cultivating a strong, positive energy within yourself that can help you stay centered and focused no matter your challenges. To that end, it's important to cultivate a regular spiritual practice that includes prayer, meditation, and other practices that help you connect with your inner self and the divine. This could involve creating a daily ritual that includes lighting candles, burning incense, and reciting prayers or mantras. It might also involve working with a particular spiritual teacher or guide who can help you deepen your spiritual practice.

Legba's Shield Bath (For Self-Protection)

Materials:
- Eucalyptus leaves
- Lemongrass

- Bay leaves
- Mint leaves
- 7 white candles
- A white cloth
- Florida water (*a sort of citrus cologne*)
- Protection oil
- A photo of yourself
- A bowl

Steps:
1. Begin by lighting the candles and placing them in a circle around you.
2. Add the eucalyptus leaves, lemongrass, bay leaves, and mint leaves to a bowl of hot water.
3. Place the bowl on the white cloth in front of you.
4. Add a few drops of Florida water and protection oil to the bowl.
5. Hold the photo of yourself in your hands and focus on your intention of protection.
6. Call upon your ancestors and ask them to bless your bath.
7. Call upon the Lwa of protection, Papa Legba, and ask for his assistance.
8. Add the photo to the bowl and stir the water with your hand.
9. Recite a protection prayer or affirmation.
10. Stand in the middle of the candle circle and pour the bathwater over your head while reciting a prayer for protection.
11. Once you have poured all the water over your head, extinguish the candles.

Fiery Shield Spell (For Self-Protection)

Materials:
- A red candle
- Dragon's Blood oil
- A photo of yourself

- A piece of red cloth
- Protection powder
- A small mirror
- A piece of black string
- A bowl

Steps:
1. Anoint the red candle with Dragon's Blood oil and place it in the center of the bowl.
2. Light the candle and focus on your desire to be safe and protected.
3. Focus on your ancestors, calling on them to bear witness to and bless this ritual.
4. Hold the photo of yourself in your hands and recite an invocation to the Lwa of protection, Papa Legba.
5. Rub the protection powder onto the red cloth and wrap it around the small mirror.
6. Tie the piece of black string around the bundle.
7. Hold the bundle in front of the lit candle and recite a prayer or affirmation for protection.
8. Place the bundle next to the candle and let the candle burn down completely.
9. Keep the bundle with you at all times for protection.

Ironclad Shield Spell (For the Protection of Someone Else)

Materials:
- A black candle
- Protection oil
- A photo of the person you wish to protect
- A piece of iron or steel
- A black cloth
- Black thread
- A bowl

Steps:
1. Anoint the black candle with protection oil and place it in the center of the bowl.
2. Light the candle and focus on your intention of protection.
3. Call upon your ancestors so they can bless and witness your ritual.
4. In your hands, hold the photo of the person you wish to protect and recite an invocation to the Lwa of protection, Ogun.
5. Place the photo in the bowl and lay the piece of iron or steel on top of it.
6. Wrap the black cloth around the bowl and tie it with the black thread.
7. Let the candle burn down completely.
8. Remove the cloth bundle from the bowl and bury it in the earth, preferably near the person you wish to protect.

Saved by Danto Spell (For Home Protection)

Materials:
- A white candle
- Protection herbs (such as bay leaves, thyme, and rosemary)
- A small bowl of salt
- A black cloth
- A piece of red string
- A photo of your home
- A bowl

Steps:
1. Light the white candle and place it in the center of the bowl.
2. Sprinkle the protection herbs around the candle.
3. Call upon your ancestors to bless your ritual.
4. Hold the photo of your home in your hands and recite an invocation to the Lwa of protection, Ezili Danto.
5. Place the photo in the bowl and sprinkle the small bowl of salt over it.
6. Wrap the black cloth around the bowl and tie it with the red string.

7. Let the candle burn down completely.
8. Remove the cloth bundle from the bowl and place it in a prominent location in your home for continued protection.

Divine Guardian Charm (To Protect Yourself or Someone Else)

Materials:
- A small white cloth
- White thread
- Protection oil
- A photo of the person you wish to protect
- Dried bay leaves
- A small white feather
- A small clear quartz crystal

Steps:
1. Begin by cutting the white cloth into a circular shape.
2. Place the photo of the person you wish to protect in the center of the cloth.
3. Call your ancestors to bless your work.
4. Add a few drops of protection oil on top of the photo.
5. Sprinkle some dried bay leaves around the photo.
6. Place the small white feather on top of the bay leaves.
7. Place the clear quartz crystal on top of the feather.
8. Gather the edges of the cloth together and tie it with the white thread.
9. Hold the charm in your hands and call upon Baron Samedi, asking for his assistance in protecting the person.
10. Invoke the person's ancestors and ask for their protection and guidance.
11. Give the charm to the person to carry with them at all times.

Sanctuary Charm (For Protecting the Home)

Materials:
- A small black cloth
- Black thread
- Protection oil
- A small jar with a lid
- Dried sage
- Dried rosemary
- A piece of black tourmaline
- Black salt

Steps:
1. Begin by cutting the black cloth into a square shape.
2. Place the dried sage and rosemary in the jar.
3. Add a few drops of protection oil on top of the herbs.
4. Place the black tourmaline in the jar.
5. Sprinkle some black salt on top of the tourmaline.
6. Close the lid of the jar tightly.
7. Wrap the jar with the black cloth and tie it with the black thread.
8. Hold the charm in your hands and call upon the Lwa of protection, Ogun, asking for his assistance in protecting the home.
9. Invoke your ancestors and ask for their protection and guidance as well.
10. Place the charm in a location within the home where it can be seen, such as on a shelf or mantelpiece.

Note that you can call on any Lwa you want whom you would prefer to protect you and that you can always substitute one material for another. You will need to refer to the glossary at the end of the book to learn what works for what.

Have You Been Hexed?

It is not uncommon for individuals who practice Voodoo to experience hexes or curses from other practitioners. A hex can cause harm and misfortune in many areas of your life, from health to career and relationships. If you suspect you have been hexed, taking immediate steps to protect yourself and reverse the curse's effects is important.

Following are several tips to help you check whether you have been hexed by another Voodoo practitioner or not, and they explain how to purge the hex and protect yourself in the future:

1. Pay attention to sudden changes in your life. If you have been experiencing a sudden string of bad luck or misfortune, it could be a sign that you have been hexed. Common signs of a hex include financial, relationship, health, and career setbacks.
2. Look for physical symptoms. A hex can also cause physical symptoms such as headaches, fatigue, and digestive issues. If you are experiencing unexplained physical symptoms, it could be a sign that you have been hexed.
3. Consult with a trusted Voodoo practitioner. If you suspect you have been hexed, seeking help from a trusted Voodoo practitioner is important. They can help you determine whether you have been hexed and guide you on reversing the curse's effects.
4. Perform a cleansing ritual. You can perform a cleansing ritual to purge the hex and cleanse yourself of negative energy. This can involve taking a bath with herbs and oils, smudging your home with sage or palo santo, or burning candles to symbolize the release of negative energy.
5. Invoke the help of a powerful Lwa. To protect yourself from future hexes, you can invoke the help of a powerful Lwa, such as Papa Legba, who is known for his ability to protect against evil and negative energy. You can offer him tobacco, rum, or coffee offerings and ask for his protection.
6. Wear protective amulets. To protect yourself from future hexes, you can wear protective amulets such as a mojo bag or a talisman made with materials such as herbs, crystals, and oils. Once made, the bag or talisman can be carried with you at all times.
7. Avoid negative people and situations. Avoiding negative people and situations that could attract negative energy is important to prevent future hexes. Surround yourself with positive people and focus on positive thoughts and actions.

8. Practice Daily Protection Rituals: Once you have had a hex removed, protecting yourself from future attacks is important. Practice daily protection rituals, such as lighting candles or carrying protective talismans. You can also create a protective mojo bag to carry with you always. Incorporate protective herbs, such as bay leaves or sage, into your home and personal space. By taking these steps, you can create a shield of protection around yourself and ward off any future attacks.

Chapter Ten: Voodoo for Love and Abundance

In the previous chapter, you learned how to perform spells, baths, rituals, and charms for protection. Now, it's time to address matters of the heart — and the pocket. The Voodooist knows they have the power to manifest these desires into their lives by creating charms. As a Voodooist, you understand that charms and spells are based on the power of intention, the beauty of creation, and the magic of the divine. So, you'll master the art of making charms, baths, and spells to open the floodgates of love and abundance in your life.

Passion Bath (For Drawing Love to You)

Materials:
- Red rose petals
- Patchouli essential oil
- Cinnamon sticks or cinnamon essential oil
- A red cloth
- A photo or personal item of the person you wish to attract
- 7 red candles
- A bowl

Steps:
1. Begin by lighting the candles and placing them in a circle around the bowl.
2. Add the red rose petals, a few drops of patchouli essential oil, and a cinnamon stick or a few drops of cinnamon essential oil to the bowl of hot water.
3. Place the bowl on the red cloth in front of you.
4. Hold the photo or personal item of the person you wish to attract in your hands and focus on your intention of attracting their love.
5. Call upon the Lwa of love and passion, Ezili Freda, and ask for her help to bring the person's love into your life.
6. Invoke your ancestors and ask for their guidance and protection.
7. Once you feel that the photo or personal item has been charged, remove it from the bowl and dry it off.
8. Step into the bath and soak for at least 20 minutes while meditating on your intention and positive affirmations.
9. Pour the remaining bathwater over the candles to extinguish them.

Self-Love Fountain Spell

Materials:
- A red or pink candle
- Rose petals
- Lavender oil
- Honey
- A small mirror
- Red or pink fabric
- Red or pink ribbon
- A piece of paper and a pen

Steps:
1. Begin by lighting the candle and placing it in front of you.
2. Write down affirmations of self-love on the piece of paper, such as "I love and accept myself just as I am" or "I radiate love and confidence."

3. Hold the mirror up to your face and recite the affirmations aloud.
4. Dip your finger in the honey and anoint the candle with it, saying, *"I am sweet, deserving, and loved."*
5. Sprinkle rose petals around the candle and drizzle a few drops of lavender oil over them.
6. Fold the paper with your affirmations and place it under the candle.
7. Wrap the candle, paper, and petals in the red or pink fabric and tie it closed with the ribbon.
8. Hold the charm to your heart and say, *"I am worthy of love, and I love myself."*
9. Ask the Lwa of love, Erzulie Freda, for her blessings and assistance in your self-love journey.
10. Keep the charm on your person or in a safe place as a reminder of your self-love intentions.

Love Drawing Spell

Materials:
- Red or pink love mojo bag
- Rose petals
- Cinnamon sticks
- Catnip
- Ginger root
- Lodestone
- A piece of paper and a pen

Steps:
1. Begin by writing down the qualities you desire in a partner on a piece of paper.
2. Fill the mojo bag with rose petals, cinnamon sticks, catnip, and ginger root.
3. Place the lodestone in the center of the herbs.
4. Fold the paper with your desired qualities and place it in the mojo bag.

5. Hold the mojo bag in your hands and recite, *"I attract the love that is true, pure, and good for me."*
6. Ask the Lwa of love and attraction, Erzili Dantor, for her assistance in manifesting your desires.
7. Keep the mojo bag on your person or in a safe place, focusing on your intentions for love and keeping an open heart.

Loving Home Spell

Materials:
- Pink or red candles (one for each member of the household)
- Vanilla oil
- Honey
- A bowl of salt
- A piece of paper and a pen

Steps:
1. Begin by lighting a pink or red candle for each household member.
2. Write down each member's name on the piece of paper and place it in the bowl of salt.
3. Anoint each candle with a drop of vanilla oil and a drizzle of honey, saying, *"May love and harmony fill our home."*
4. Light each candle and sprinkle a pinch of salt over the flame, saying, *"May negativity and discord be banished from our home."*
5. Hold hands with your family members as the candles burn and recite a prayer or affirmation for love and unity.
6. Ask the Lwa you've chosen for their blessings and protection over your household.
7. Allow the candles to burn down completely or snuff them out with a snuffer, but never blow them out.
8. Dispose of the salt and paper by burying them outside of your home.

Note: It is important to perform this spell with the consent and participation of all household members.

Golden Opportunity Charm

Materials:
- A small golden coin or charm
- A green or gold drawstring bag
- Cinnamon sticks
- Bay leaves
- Cloves
- Allspice berries

Steps:
1. Begin by invoking the Lwa of prosperity, Ayizan, and calling on your ancestors for their guidance and blessings.
2. Hold the golden coin or charm in your hands and visualize yourself receiving abundance and financial opportunities.
3. Place the coin or charm into the green or gold drawstring bag.
4. Add in the cinnamon sticks, bay leaves, cloves, and allspice berries.
5. Close the bag and shake it gently, saying, "*Opportunities come my way; prosperity is here to stay.*"
6. Carry the charm with you, or keep it in a safe place in your home or office.

Wealthy Path Charm

Materials:
- A small green cloth or sachet
- A dollar bill or other currency
- Peppermint leaves
- Alfalfa
- Pyrite crystal
- A small gold-colored charm or trinket

Steps:
1. Begin by invoking Damballa and calling on your ancestors for guidance and blessings.

2. Place the dollar bill or currency in the center of the green cloth or sachet.
3. Add in the peppermint leaves and alfalfa.
4. Place the pyrite crystal on top of the dollar bill or currency.
5. Add the small gold-colored charm or trinket.
6. Tie up the cloth or sachet with a gold ribbon or string, saying, *"Wealth and prosperity come my way, blessings for me every day."*
7. Keep the charm with you, or place it in a prominent location in your home or office.

Success and Prosperity Charm

Materials:
- A small red or gold bag
- Three cinnamon sticks
- Allspice berries
- Bay leaves
- A small piece of citrine crystal

Steps:
1. Begin by invoking the Lwa of opportunity, Papa Legba, and calling on your ancestors for their guidance and blessings.
2. Place the cinnamon sticks, allspice berries, and bay leaves into the red or gold bag.
3. Add the citrine crystal to the bag.
4. Hold the bag in your hands and visualize yourself achieving success and prosperity in your business or career.
5. Tie up the bag with a red or gold ribbon or string, saying, *"Success and prosperity come my way; blessings for me every day."*
6. Keep the charm with you, or place it in a prominent location in your office or workspace.

Gold Fortune Bath

Materials:
- Bay leaves
- Cinnamon sticks
- Dried chamomile flowers
- Gold glitter
- Honey
- Coconut milk
- Yellow candle
- Bathtub

Steps:
1. Light the yellow candle and place it near the bathtub.
2. Add a handful of bay leaves, a few cinnamon sticks, and a small amount of dried chamomile flowers to the bathwater.
3. Add a pinch of gold glitter and a tablespoon of honey to the bathwater.
4. Pour in a can of coconut milk and mix everything together.
5. Soak in the bath, visualizing yourself surrounded by golden light and abundance.
6. Invoke the Lwa of prosperity, Erzili Freda, by saying, *"Erzili Freda, please bless me with your love and abundance."*
7. Invoke your ancestors by saying, *"Ancestors, please guide and protect me on my path to prosperity."*

Fortunate Business Bath

Materials:
- Green tea bags
- Dried basil leaves
- Dried rosemary
- Green glitter
- Patchouli oil

- Green candle
- Bathtub

Steps:
1. Light the green candle and place it near the bathtub.
2. Add 2-3 green tea bags, a handful of dried basil leaves, and a few dried rosemary sprigs to the bathwater.
3. Add a pinch of green glitter and a few drops of patchouli oil to the bathwater.
4. Soak in the bath, visualizing success and abundance in your business or career.
5. Invoke Papa Legba by saying, *"Papa Legba, please open the gates to success and prosperity in my business/career."*
6. Invoke your ancestors by saying, *"Ancestors, please guide and protect me on my path to financial success."*

Be Prosperous Bath

Materials:
- Dried lavender
- Dried chamomile flowers
- Honey
- White candle
- Bathtub

Steps:
1. Light the white candle and place it near the bathtub.
2. Add a handful of dried lavender and a small amount of dried chamomile flowers to the bathwater.
3. Add a tablespoon of honey to the bathwater.
4. Soak in the bath, visualizing abundance and prosperity for the person you wish to help.
5. Invoke Loko by saying, *"Loko, please bless (person's name) with abundance and prosperity."*
6. Invoke your ancestors by saying, *"Ancestors, please guide and protect (person's name) on their path to prosperity."*

Crafting Your Own Rituals

Voodoo rituals are a powerful and sacred practice that requires careful preparation and execution. To create a successful and effective ritual, it's important to understand the general structure that most Voodoo rituals follow. Voodoo rituals are usually divided into four stages:

- Preparation
- Invocation
- Possession
- Farewell

The first stage, preparation, is crucial to the ritual's success. During this stage, the practitioner will gather all of the materials they need for the ritual, including herbs, candles, and other tools. They will also prepare the physical space where the ritual will take place. This may involve setting up an altar or other sacred space and cleansing and purifying the area to remove any negative energy or entities.

In the second stage, invocation, the practitioner calls upon the spirits and deities to aid them in their work. This is typically done through prayers, invocations, and offerings, such as food or drink. During this stage, the practitioner may also make requests or petitions to the spirits or deities for specific outcomes or blessings.

In the third stage, possession, the practitioner may enter a trance state and become possessed by the spirits or deities. This can be a powerful and transformative experience, allowing the practitioner to gain insights and receive guidance from the spirits. During possession, the practitioner may speak in tongues, dance, or physically express the spirits' presence. In your personal rituals, this can simply be you feeling the energy of the Lwa in and around you.

In the final stage, the practitioner bids farewell to the spirits and deities and releases them from the physical space. This may involve offering thanks and gratitude for their assistance and cleansing and purifying the area again to remove any lingering energy or entities. It's important to note that not all Voodoo rituals will follow this exact structure, and different practitioners may have their own variations and methods. However, understanding the general structure can provide a helpful framework for creating your own rituals or participating in those led by others.

In addition to the four stages, it's also important to consider the intention and energy behind the ritual. The practitioner should approach the ritual with a clear and focused intention and strongly believe in the power of the spirits and deities to assist them in their work. They should also be respectful and mindful of the spirits and deities, offering gratitude and honor for their assistance.

Glossary

In Voodoo, you need certain materials to be able to carry out your spells, venerate your ancestors and Loa, and work your magic. These materials are typically herbs and roots, candles, and oils. You will need to know the spiritual significance of each of these items, and that's why this glossary has been written to give you just that information.

Herbs and Roots

Angelica Root - provides strength, protection, and good luck. It is used in protection and healing spells.

Anise - brings protection, purification, and psychic abilities. It is used in divination and protection spells.

Basil - attracts prosperity, love, and peace. It is used in love and money spells.

Bay Leaf - provides protection, purification, and success. This is used in protection and wish spells.

Black Cohosh - brings power, strength, and protection. This is used in hex-breaking and protection spells.

Calamus Root - brings luck, money, and healing. This is used in spells for success and good fortune.

Camphor - repels negativity and evil. This is used in purification and protection spells.

Cinnamon - brings success, prosperity, and love. This is used in money and love spells.

Cloves - provide protection, healing, and love. This is used in protection and love spells.

Comfrey Root - brings safety, protection, and healing. This is used in spells for safety and protection.

Dragon's Blood - enhances power and success. This is used in spells for protection and empowerment.

Eucalyptus - brings healing and purification; used in healing and cleansing spells.

Fennel - enhances psychic abilities and brings protection. This is used in divination and protection spells.

Frankincense - provides protection, purification, and spiritual growth. This is used in purification and protection spells.

Galangal Root - brings good luck, love, and protection and is used in love and protection spells.

Ginger - enhances power and success and is used in spells for success and good fortune.

Hawthorn Berry - provides protection, purification, and good luck and is used in protection and healing spells.

Hyssop - brings purification and protection and is used in purification and protection spells.

Jasmine - enhances psychic abilities and love and can be used in love and divination spells.

Juniper Berries - brings purification and protection and can be used in purification and protection spells.

Lavender - brings calmness, love, and purification and is used in love and purification spells.

Lemon Balm - brings love and success and is used in love and success spells.

Lemongrass - brings purification, love, and healing and is used in purification and love spells.

Licorice Root - enhances power and success and is often used in spells for success and good fortune.

Mandrake Root - enhances power and protection and is used in spells for protection and empowerment.

Mint - brings prosperity, healing, and protection and is used in money and healing spells.

Mugwort - enhances psychic abilities and brings protection and is often used in divination and protection spells.

Myrrh - provides purification, protection, and spiritual growth and is used in purification and protection spells.

Nettle - brings protection, healing, and purification and is used in protection and healing spells.

Orange Peel - enhances love and brings good luck and is used in love and luck spells.

Patchouli - enhances love, prosperity, and protection and is used in love and money spells.

Peppermint - brings prosperity, healing, and protection and is used in money and healing spells.

Pine - brings purification, protection, and healing and can be used in purification and healing spells.

Red Pepper - brings protection and good luck and is often used in protection and money spells.

Rose - enhances love and brings healing and is commonly used in love and healing spells.

Rosemary - brings purification, protection, and love and is used in purification and love spells.

Sandalwood - enhances spirituality, brings calmness and clarity, and is used in meditation and purification spells.

Sarsaparilla Root - provides protection and enhances sexual potency and is often used in protection and love spells.

Solomon's Seal Root - brings protection and healing and can be used in protection and healing spells.

St. John's Wort - brings happiness, protection, and purification. This can be used in protection and purification spells.

Thyme - brings purification, courage, and psychic abilities. It is used in purification and courage spells.

Valerian Root - enhances love, brings calmness and sleep, and can be used in love and sleep spells.

Vervain - enhances spirituality, brings protection and purification, and is used in purification and protection spells.

Vetiver - enhances love and brings grounding and protection - often used in love and protection spells.

White Sage - brings purification and protection and can be used in purification and protection spells.

Wormwood - enhances psychic abilities and brings protection and can be used in divination and protection spells.

Yarrow - brings courage, protection, and love – often used in courage and love spells.

Yerba Santa - brings purification, healing, and protection and is used in purification and healing spells.

Yucca Root - enhances spiritual power, brings protection and prosperity, it is used in protection and money spells.

Note: In Voodoo, herbs and roots play a significant role in the practice of magic, as they are believed to possess spiritual properties that can aid in spells and rituals. The herbs and roots listed above have different spiritual meanings, roles, and uses in spells. Some are used for protection, purification, and healing, while others are used for love, prosperity, and success. When using herbs and roots in spells, it is essential to understand their properties and how they can be incorporated into the spell. Some herbs may be burned, brewed in tea, carried in a sachet, or used in a bath. The choice of which herb or root you use may also depend on the goal of the spell and be relevant to the specific Lwa or ancestor being invoked. It is important to note that while herbs and roots can be potent aids in spells and rituals, they are not a replacement for professional medical or legal advice. Voodoo is a powerful and complex spiritual practice, and it should be approached with respect, understanding, and caution.

Oils

African Musk Oil - brings protection, love, and prosperity and is used in love and money spells.

Allspice Oil - enhances power and success and can be used in spells for success and good fortune.

Amber Oil - provides protection and attracts love. Thus, it is used in protection and love spells.

Anise Oil - brings purification, psychic abilities, and protection. This is used in divination and protection spells.

Basil Oil - attracts prosperity, love, and peace. Often it is used in love and money spells.

Bayberry Oil - brings prosperity and abundance. It is used in money and prosperity spells.

Benzoin Oil - provides purification, protection, and spiritual growth. This is used in purification and protection spells.

Black Pepper Oil - brings protection, purification, and success. It is used in protection and success spells.

Calamus Oil - brings good luck, money, and healing and is used in spells for success and good fortune.

Camphor Oil - repels negativity and evil; and is used in purification and protection spells.

Cardamom Oil - enhances love and brings good luck and is used in love and luck spells.

Cedarwood Oil - brings purification, protection, and healing and can be used in purification and healing spells.

Chamomile Oil - brings love and purification and is used in love and purification spells.

Cinnamon Oil - brings success, prosperity, and love and is used in money and love spells.

Citronella Oil - repels negativity and evil and can be used in purification and protection spells.

Clove Oil - provides protection, healing, and love and is often used in protection and love spells.

Coconut Oil - brings purification, protection, and success and is used in purification and success spells.

Eucalyptus Oil - brings healing and purification and is thus used in healing and cleansing spells.

Frankincense Oil - provides protection, purification, and spiritual growth and is used in purification and protection spells.

Gardenia Oil - enhances love and brings success, often used in love and success spells.

Ginger Oil - enhances power and success and is used in spells for success and good fortune.

Grapefruit Oil - brings purification and healing and is thus used in purification and healing spells.

Jasmine Oil - enhances psychic abilities and love and can be used in love and divination spells.

Lavender Oil - brings calmness, love, and purification and is sometimes used in love and purification spells.

Lemongrass Oil - brings purification, love, and healing and is used in purification and love spells.

Lime Oil - brings purification and protection and is used in purification and protection spells.

Lotus Oil - enhances spiritual growth and brings love and is used in spiritual and love spells.

Magnolia Oil - enhances love and brings good luck and is used in love and luck spells.

Myrrh Oil - provides purification, protection, and spiritual growth and can be used in purification and protection spells

Neroli Oil - enhances love and brings purification. It is used in love and purification spells.

Orange Oil - brings purification and enhances love. It is used in purification and love spells.

Patchouli Oil - enhances love, prosperity, and protection and is often used in love and money spells.

Peppermint Oil - brings prosperity, healing, and protection. It is used in money and healing spells.

Pine Oil - brings purification, protection, and healing. It is used in purification and healing spells.

Rose Oil - enhances love and brings healing and is used in love and healing spells.

Rosemary Oil - brings purification, protection, and love and is often used in purification and love spells.

Rue Oil - provides protection, purification, and healing and is used in protection and purification spells.

Sandalwood Oil - enhances spiritual growth, protection, and healing and is used in spiritual and healing spells.

Spearmint Oil - brings healing and purification and can be used in healing and purification spells.

Sweetgrass Oil - enhances spiritual growth and brings purification and is used in spiritual and purification spells.

Tangerine Oil - enhances love and brings purification and is therefore used in love and purification spells.

Tea Tree Oil - brings healing and protection and is used in healing and protection spells.

Thyme Oil - enhances psychic abilities and brings purification and is used in divination and purification spells.

Vanilla Oil - enhances love and brings good luck and is used in love and luck spells.

Vetiver Oil - enhances protection, purification, and grounding. This is used in protection and purification spells.

Wisteria Oil - enhances psychic abilities and brings success. This is used in divination and success spells.

Yarrow Oil - enhances psychic abilities and brings love. It is often used in divination and love spells.

Ylang Ylang Oil - enhances love and brings purification. It is used in love and purification spells.

Zedoary Oil - brings purification and enhances psychic abilities. This is used in purification and divination spells.

Please note that these oils and their corresponding spiritual meanings, roles, and usages may vary depending on the practitioner and tradition of Voodoo. It is important to always research and consult with a trusted and experienced practitioner before using any oils or conducting any spells.

Candles

Candles are an important tool in Voodoo rituals and spells. They are often used to focus the practitioner's intention and provide a physical representation of the energy directed towards a particular goal or outcome. The candle color used in a spell can play an important role in its effectiveness, as each color is associated with a particular intention or energy. Here are some common candle colors used in Voodoo, along with their meanings and spiritual uses:

White: purity, clarity, healing, and protection. White candles can be used for any purpose, as they represent the purest and most neutral form of energy.

Black: banishing, protecting, and breaking curses. Black candles are often used in spells to remove negative energy or protect against harm.

Red: love, passion, strength, and courage. Red candles can be used in spells related to romantic love, as well as to boost personal power and confidence.

Pink: love, friendship, and emotional healing. Pink candles are often used in spells related to emotional healing, self-love, and friendship.

Blue: calmness, communication, and healing. Blue candles can be used in spells related to clear communication, peacefulness, and emotional healing.

Green: abundance, prosperity, and growth. Green candles can be used in spells related to money, success, and personal growth.

Yellow: clarity, intellect, and creativity. Yellow candles can be used in spells related to mental clarity, focus, and creativity.

Purple: spiritual power, intuition, and psychic abilities. Purple candles can be used in spells related to spiritual growth, psychic abilities, and intuition.

Orange: energy, enthusiasm, and success. Orange candles can be used in spells related to success, enthusiasm, and increased energy.

In addition to the different colors, there are also different types of candles used in Voodoo. Some practitioners prefer to use beeswax candles, as they are considered to be more natural and powerful than other types of candles. Some also prefer to use tapered candles, which can be carved with symbols or inscriptions related to the intended outcome of the spell.

Disclaimer: Whatever you do, please do not ingest any oils or herbs, as they can be dangerous. When applying oil to the skin, please do a patch test first by applying a small amount on the inner part of your wrist and then wait a day to see if you have any adverse reaction. Please note that you should keep your herbs, roots, and oils away from children and pets so they don't hurt themselves. Store them safely away where only you can reach them.

Conclusion

You have reached the end of "Voodoo for Beginners - A guide to New Orleans Voodoo, Haitian Vodou, and Hoodoo." Thank you for taking the time to read this book and explore Voodoo's rich and fascinating world. Throughout this book, you have gained an understanding of Voodoo's history, beliefs, practices, and traditions. You have learned about the differences between New Orleans Voodoo, Haitian Vodou, and Hoodoo and how each of these practices can be used to help you achieve your desires and goals.

You have discovered the importance of connecting with ancestors and spirits and how to work with them to manifest positive change in your life. Remember, the core principles of Voodoo are faith, respect, and gratitude. When you approach this practice with an open mind and heart and with the intention to help yourself and others, you will be rewarded with powerful spiritual experiences and meaningful connections.

As you begin to incorporate the practices and rituals of Voodoo into your daily life, remember that consistency and dedication are key. The more you practice, the stronger your connection with the spirits and ancestors will become, and the more effective your spells and rituals will be. It is also important to continue your studies and seek out guidance from those who have practiced longer than you have. Attend local Voodoo ceremonies and events, and connect with others who share your interest in this spiritual practice. There is always more to learn; by seeking new knowledge and experiences, you will continue to grow and evolve in your practice.

Finally, remember that Voodoo is a powerful tool for personal growth and transformation, but it is not a substitute for professional help. Suppose you are experiencing serious physical, emotional, or mental health issues. In that case, it is important to seek the advice and guidance of a qualified medical or mental health professional. In closing, may you continue to explore this fascinating and powerful spiritual practice with an open mind and heart, and may the spirits and ancestors guide and bless you on your path.

Part 2: New Orleans Voodoo

An Essential Guide to Louisiana Voodoo

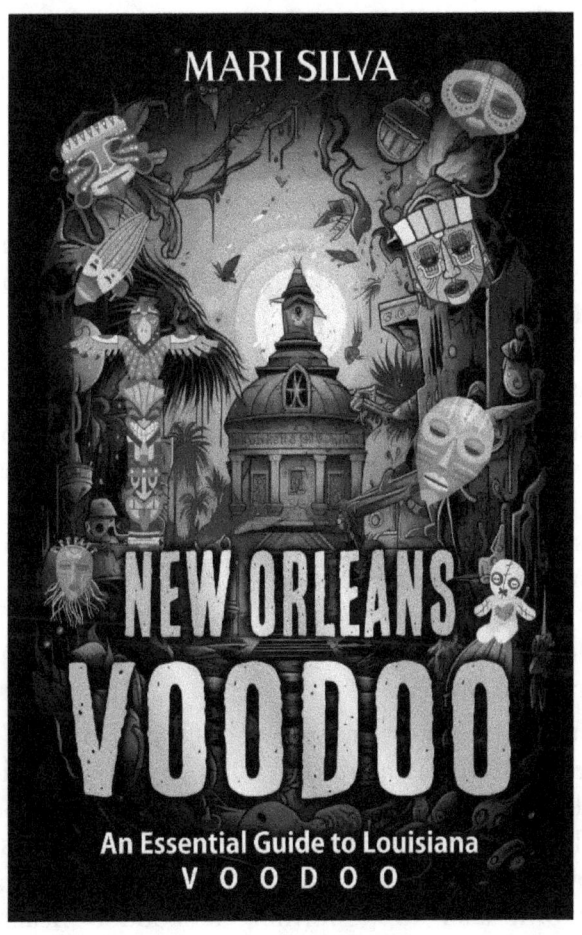

Introduction

New Orleans Voodoo is a practice that has been shrouded in mystery and misconceptions for years. It is rather unfortunate that for many, the term Voodoo evokes images of black magic and human sacrifice, but the reality is that New Orleans Voodoo is a complex spiritual tradition with deep roots in the history and culture of Louisiana.

In this essential guide to Louisiana Voodoo, you're going to gain a deeper understanding of this powerful and often misunderstood practice. The book is perfect for both beginners who are just getting their feet wet when it comes to the powerful practice of New Orleans Voodoo and those who have some knowledge of Voodoo but want to delve deeper into their exploration of the tradition. You'll find this book is written in a clear and accessible style, making it easy to understand and follow along with the various practices and rituals.

There are many books on the subject out there, but you'll be glad you chose this one. What sets it apart from other similar guides is its hands-on approach. Rather than simply explaining the history and beliefs of New Orleans Voodoo, the book includes step-by-step instructions and practical advice on how to engage with the various rituals and practices. From creating your own altar to performing a Voodoo healing ceremony, readers will have everything they need to start their own Voodoo practice.

Another unique aspect of this book is its focus on the role of New Orleans in the development and spread of Voodoo. The city has long been a hub for spiritual practices and has played a vital role in preserving and evolving Voodoo in America. The book delves into the history of

New Orleans and its various spiritual traditions, showing how Voodoo fits into this rich tapestry.

You will encounter the various spirits and deities central to New Orleans Voodoo. These include the powerful Loa, or spirits, which you can call upon for guidance, protection, and healing. The book explains the different types of Loa and their roles within the Voodoo tradition and provides guidance on how to work with them.

If you've always wanted a way to connect with the Divine, to deepen your roots in spirituality so that you can live a life with purpose and clarity, then this is definitely the path for you. It's not for those only looking to "curate" their lives to fit what they consider "aesthetic." It's for those who want to know the ancient ways, divine truths, and natural ways to live in harmony with one another. You'll discover all this and more as you read this book. If you're ready for your new spiritual journey, let's get into it.

Chapter One: What Makes New Orleans Voodoo Different?

Beliefs

West Africa is the cradle from which Voodoo sprung and grew. The word *voodoo* itself came about in Louisiana in 1850 and is considered a derivative of the French word *voudou*. Some say it's from the word *vodu*. You may find it spelled in a variety of other ways, like vodun, vodou, and so on.

For many reasons, the uninitiated or ignorant consider Voodoo to be the practice of black magic. Say the word "*Voodoo,*" and it immediately brings to mind things like cursing people or sticking pins into a doll. But this is just a misrepresentation. Voodoo is all about the awareness that all things and all people are made of the same essence or Spirit. Therefore, everything is connected.

While Voodoo is from West Africa, it is rooted in Catholicism. As a syncretic religion, it is a mix of belief systems drawn from the Catholic Church and the West African Vodu ways. One of the fundamental ideas behind Voodoo is the fact that humans live in a world with spirits all around them. Humans aren't the only ones here. There are spirits known as Loa or Lwa, as well as the ancestors and angels, all of whom inhabit the worlds that cannot be seen with the naked eye. These spirits are so numerous that the Loa alone can be split into 17 pantheons, and there are over a thousand of them — some, admittedly more well-known than others.

Voodoo is rooted in Catholicism.[14]

According to Voodoo, all the spirits dwell in Ginen, and they were all made by Bondye, the Supreme Being who created all things seen and unseen. The purpose of these spirits is simple. They're supposed to act as assistants to Bondye, seeing to the affairs of the outside world. Not only that, but no one also gets to interact with Bondye directly other than these spirits. Therefore, if you have any petitions or prayers, they must go through the Loa. This isn't because Bondye doesn't care, but simply because the essence of Bondye is so different from humanity that the only way to communicate clearly and accurately with him is through the help of the Loa.

The practice of Voodoo isn't just something done now and then. It is a lifestyle, an awareness that each day is dedicated to the service of the Loa. Many practices are involved in this service, such as rites, rituals, special prayers, offerings, and more. These are all meant to get the Loa as involved in your daily affairs as possible, so they can bless you, help you figure out problems, keep you safe and healthy, and more. Those who practice Voodoo will dance and sing in honor of the Loa, and they also get into altered states of consciousness where the Loa themselves will possess them and use them to transmit messages or just demonstrate their presence to the people. Possession also allows those who practice Voodoo to receive specific advice when needed.

Voodoo is a religious belief system rooted in spirituality and considers the ancestors to be an important aspect of life. Before analyzing what makes New Orleans Voodoo different from other forms of Voodoo, it is important to have a clear picture of the background of this amazing spiritual movement. So, here's a deep dive into the history and culture that led to the development of New Orleans Voodoo as it is known today.

Historical and Cultural Background

When it comes to Louisiana Voodoo, there is a lot of mystery shrouding its roots. In the year 1699, some French people arrived in the area and settled down. About 20 years later, the area would receive enslaved African people. Things remained relatively unchanged for over 40 years until the Spanish Empire stepped in and took over. They held the reins of power up until 1803. At this time, there was a synchronization of Catholicism that was the practice of the Spanish and the French, as well as the religions among those who had been enslaved in West Africa, and this served as the fertile ground from which Voodoo would spring.

All the people forced to leave West Africa knew a lot about various poisons, plants, herbal solutions, amulets, rituals, charms, and more. These were all used to keep themselves safe, and they would all eventually become a part of Louisiana or New Orleans Voodoo. When the French held sway, most Africans there were from the Senegal River basin. Specifically, they were of the Bambara tribe. There were other tribes as well, including the Dahomey people and the Kongolese. After the Spanish wrested power from the French, there were more and more Kongolese enslaved people. Naturally, there were soon far more enslaved people than white Europeans. Even before the enslaved people got there, the colony wasn't exactly a bastion of excellence and efficiency. Consequently, those who had only just arrived from sub-Saharan Africa would end up taking over the slave community.

Between 1731 and 1732, there were at least two African people for every European. Those Europeans involved in agriculture and the slave business weren't that great in number. One of the things that made it easier for Africans to prevent their culture from being overly diluted was the fact that the white people had ensured they would never interact with the Africans unless necessary. So this made it easier for the latter group to keep their culture as untainted as they could. This was more common in southern Louisiana than in the northern part of the state.

Because of Catholicism and the laws put in place by the French, it wasn't allowed to sell children of enslaved people off to other families if they weren't at least 14 years old. Since the people weren't being separated to be sold off, this made it easier for the bond between them to grow stronger, in addition to sharing a mutual understanding of what it's like not to have freedom.

An important part of New Orleans Voodoo is wearing amulets and other objects to stay safe from the elements and other people and heal themselves of any illnesses. For instance, there was the Ouanga, a potent charm that could be used on an enemy to poison them. Part of the ingredients for this charm were roots obtained from the African *figuier maudit* tree.

Eventually, Louisiana would come to be the property of the United States in the year 1803. This was around the time that the Africans in Saint-Domingue rose up to rid themselves of the terrorizing French colonials so that they could become the republic known today as Haiti. Some people chose to escape the war there and made their homes in Louisiana. They came with all they had, and that included Haitian Vodou, which was a result of the syncretization of Yoruba and Fon religious practices, as well as Roman Catholic ones. Enough people migrated so that New Orleans' population doubled; as they interacted with one another, many born in Louisiana chose to practice Voodoo. Not only that, but they also found a way to blend their practices with Haitian Voodoo, creating Louisiana Voodoo as it is known today. At this point in Louisiana Voodoo's history, it is important to look into the other branches of Voodoo that exist so that it's easier to demonstrate how these various branches differ from New Orleans Voodoo.

The Different Branches of Voodoo

Haitian Voodoo: Haitian Voodoo is perhaps the most well-known and widely practiced form in the Western world. It is a syncretic religion that combines elements of traditional West African religions, Catholicism, and indigenous beliefs. Haitian Voodoo is characterized by the veneration of ancestors, the use of spirit possession in rituals, and the use of drumming and dance as part of its religious practices. The religion also has a complex system of spirits, known as Lwa (Loa), who are believed to represent various aspects of the natural world and human experience.

A Haitian Voodoo altar.[15]

African Voudou: African Voudou, on the other hand, is the oldest and most traditional form of Voodoo, with deep roots in West African cultures. It is a nature-based religion centered on worshiping deities known as Orishas, who represent various natural elements and forces. African Voudou emphasizes the importance of ancestor veneration, healing, and divination. Its rituals involve chanting, dancing, and drumming. Its practitioners often wear elaborate costumes and use symbolic objects during their ceremonies.

Hoodoo: Hoodoo, also known as "rootwork," is a practice of African American folk magic combining elements of African spirituality with Christian beliefs. Hoodoo practitioners use herbs, oils, and other ingredients to create potions and charms for various purposes, such as love, protection, and success. Hoodoo also incorporates divination and other forms of magic into its practice.

Louisiana Voodoo: Also called New Orleans Voodoo, this form developed in New Orleans. New Orleans Voodoo is a blend of African, European, and Native American spiritual traditions. It includes the worship of spirits, ancestor veneration, and the use of charms and spells. *You're going to learn more about this form in this book.*

Brazilian Vodou: Brazilian Vodou is also known as Candomblé. This is a religion that developed in Brazil and is heavily influenced by African spiritual practices. Brazilian Vodou involves the worship of Orishas, or deities, and includes a range of rituals and ceremonies.

Dominican Vodou: Also known as Las 21 Divisiones, Dominican Vodou is a form of Voodoo practiced in the Dominican Republic. Dominican Vodou involves the worship of spirits and includes a range of rituals and ceremonies.

Cuban Santeria: Cuban Santeria is sometimes called Lukumi. This is a religion that developed in Cuba and which is heavily influenced by African spiritual practices. Cuban Santeria involves the worship of Orishas, or deities, and includes a range of rituals and ceremonies.

When it comes to practicing all these forms of Vodou, personal beliefs also come into play, and, as a result, some people blend practices from the different forms of Vodou to create what resonates with them spiritually.

The Evolution of New Orleans Voodoo

It was only natural that, with time, New Orleans Voodoo would evolve to become something different, a conglomeration of different beliefs and practices from many spiritual traditions. Hoodoo, for instance, is a form of magic from South America. We can clearly find its fingerprints all over New Orleans Voodoo these days.

New Orleans Voodoo is still practiced because it is a true form of spirituality that connects you with the divine within and all around you. Many following this path are from the original Voodoo practitioners responsible for the religion. There are, however, a growing number of people who are not from New Orleans and do not have any connections with Voodoo but are very interested in the path. Some people are naturally drawn to it, so New Orleans Voodoo continues to spread. This is such a wonderful thing because, in the past, Voodoo was something most people demonized. These days, many people have come to not just recognize but accept it as a valid part of the culture of New Orleans.

When you consider the entire evolution of New Orleans Voodoo, it is hard to ignore the fact that it has continued to grow and adapt to the times and the beliefs of present-day practitioners. This spiritual way of life remains an intrinsic part of the city of New Orleans. The locals and visitors appreciate all its practices, history, and endurance.

Myths, Misconceptions, and Malicious Lies

It is a sad truth that once upon a time, Voodoo was heavily vilified, especially in popular culture. Many erroneously assumed that Voodoo was the same as evil black magic witchcraft or anything dark that one should not dabble with. The vilification of Voodoo is no accident. Some were deeply interested in discrediting Voodoo because of what they thought it stood for.

One of the major reasons that Voodoo is so misunderstood is because of its connection to the continent of Africa and the diaspora. You see, earlier in the 19th and 20th centuries, when Voodoo first became a thing in the Western world, many people had a terrible attitude towards people from Africa and their cultures. It was a time when racism and xenophobia reigned supreme. Looking through those lenses, those people naturally assumed that everything to do with Voodoo was barbaric and primitive. Anything and anyone associated with the practice was seen as ignorant. To these people, practitioners of Voodoo were savages. Therefore, ensuring this religion would not thrive and become a blemish upon their already established and lawful customs and cultures became very important to them.

Yet another incentive why these people had to vilify Voodoo is the fact that this religion is closely associated with the spirit of freedom, social unrest, and rebellion against the powers that be. The colonizers at this time were deeply afraid of the effects of the unification that could be found in the practice of this religion. Rightfully so, because Voodoo became a tool to fuel resistance against oppression and finally secure the enslaved African peoples' freedom. Knowing this caused the colonialists to put all of their resources into making sure that this religion would be demonized to keep the enslaved people from dissenting or resisting their rule.

The erroneous assumptions of the ignorant about Voodoo are further fueled by how Hollywood represents it. Hollywood and popular culture have played a significant role in perpetuating negative stereotypes about Voodoo. In many movies and television shows, Voodoo is portrayed as a dark and mysterious practice associated with evil spirits, black magic, and human sacrifice. This depiction of Voodoo is often sensationalized and exaggerated; it does not accurately represent the true nature of the religion.

Another reason for the misrepresentation of Voodoo in popular culture is the influence of religious and cultural biases. Many Western societies have a history of demonizing non-Christian religions, particularly those practiced by enslaved or colonized peoples. In the case of Voodoo, this bias has led to the spread of false and negative beliefs about religion. Despite these misconceptions, Voodoo is a deeply spiritual and empowering religion emphasizing personal growth, community, and connection with the natural world. Its practices and beliefs are based on a deep reverence for ancestors, nature, and the divine. Its rituals and ceremonies are designed to connect practitioners with these powerful spiritual forces.

In recent years, there has been a growing interest in Voodoo as a legitimate spiritual practice. Efforts are being made to reclaim its rightful place as a powerful and transformative religion. Through education, cultural exchange, and greater representation in popular media, many practitioners are working to dispel the myths and misconceptions that have long plagued the religion and to celebrate its rich history and enduring legacy of revolution, freedom, and spiritual enlightenment.

Madame Laveau

Madame Laveau, the Voodoo Queen of New Orleans, was a powerful figure in Louisiana Voodoo. Her legacy is a testament to the enduring power of this spiritual tradition and the people who practice it. Born in 1801, Madame Laveau was a woman of remarkable strength and resilience. She rose to prominence in the early 19th century as a leader of the Voodoo community in New Orleans. Her knowledge of the rituals and practices of Voodoo was unparalleled, and her followers revered her for her ability to heal the sick and cast powerful spells.

This powerful woman's influence extended far beyond the Voodoo community. She was a respected figure in New Orleans society and was known for her acts of charity and kindness. She used her position of power to advocate for marginalized people's rights and fight against the injustices of the time. Madame Laveau's impact on Louisiana Voodoo was profound. She helped to shape the rituals and practices of the tradition, and her legacy continues to inspire Voodoo practitioners to this day. Her reputation as a powerful conjurer and healer has made her a legendary figure in the world of Voodoo, and her spirit is said to still be present in New Orleans. You could say that her life and legacy are a testament to the power of Voodoo and its ability to transform lives. She was a true pioneer and a visionary, and her contributions to the tradition will never be forgotten.

Dr. John

Dr. John, the Voodoo practitioner, was known for his deep roots in Louisiana Voodoo. He was a master of the mystical arts and a powerful practitioner of the rituals and spells that are at the heart of this complex spiritual tradition. Through his music, Dr. John brought the magic and mystery of Louisiana Voodoo to a wider audience. He infused his songs with the rhythms and incantations of the Voodoo ceremonies that he had witnessed and participated in throughout his life. He drew upon the spiritual traditions of his ancestors and the teachings of his mentors to create a unique and powerful expression that resonated with audiences worldwide.

Dr. John was a skilled practitioner of the Voodoo arts and was respected by the Voodoo community in New Orleans and beyond. He was known for performing powerful spells and healing the sick and suffering using herbs, oils, and other natural remedies. In addition to his musical and spiritual contributions, Dr. John was also a champion of the cultural heritage of Louisiana and its people. He was a tireless advocate for the preservation of the unique traditions and customs of the region, including Voodoo. He worked to ensure that they would be passed down to future generations.

This man's influence on Louisiana Voodoo and the broader cultural landscape of New Orleans cannot be overstated. He was a true visionary and a master of his craft, and his legacy will continue to inspire and guide people for generations to come. The doctor was a remarkable figure who wove the threads of the mystical and the music into a singular tapestry. He was born in New Orleans, Louisiana, in the early 20th century and grew up in the heart of the city's rich cultural gumbo. He came to be known as "Dr. John" after the Voodoo priest of the same name who lived in the 19th century. He was a master of the piano, a true bluesman who played with soul and passion. He infused his music with the rhythms of his beloved New Orleans, the African diaspora, and the sounds of the bayou.

Dr. John's music was not only a celebration of the rich cultural heritage of New Orleans but also a potent expression of the human experience. He sang of love, heartache, joy, and sorrow. He was a storyteller, a bard who wove tales of the people and places he knew so well. Dr. John's legacy lives on through his music and the many lives that he touched. He was a visionary, a pioneer, and a true original. His artistry was a testament to the power of the human spirit, and his life was a testament to the transformative power of music.

Chapter Two: Getting Ready for Voodoo

So, you want to serve the Loa, but there's a big question that's been bothering you. You're wondering if it's okay to just up and start Voodoo right away, head first, with no preparation. Well, the first thing you need to understand is if you truly want to practice this, you've got to be initiated.

Voodoo dolls.[16]

The Importance of Formal Initiation

The importance of initiation in Voodoo cannot be overstated. It is a sacred religion that demands deep respect and reverence. It cannot be taken lightly or approached without the proper guidance and training. In Voodoo, priests and priestesses are known respectively as houngans and mambos. These individuals have been initiated into the religion and have undergone a rigorous process of training and study. They hold a deep understanding of the practices and traditions of Voodoo and can guide practitioners through the initiation process.

To find true houngans and mambos, it is important to do your research and be cautious. Unfortunately, some try to scam individuals by pretending to be Voodoo practitioners. These individuals often make unrealistic promises or ask for large sums of money in exchange for their services. It is essential to be wary of such individuals and to seek out legitimate practitioners. One way to tell if a houngan or mambo is the real deal is to look for recommendations from other Voodoo community practitioners or members. You can also seek out individuals who have been practicing for many years and have a deep knowledge of the practices and traditions of the religion. A true houngan or mambo will also be respectful and cautious in their approach and will not promise unrealistic results.

The requirements for initiation into Voodoo can vary depending on the house or community. In general, however, it involves a process of training, study, and ritual. This can include learning about the history and traditions of the religion, developing a relationship with spirits and ancestors, and participating in ritual practices. It is a deeply personal and spiritual journey that requires dedication and commitment. By seeking out true houngans and mambos and undergoing the initiation process, you can develop a deep understanding and appreciation of the practices and traditions of Voodoo. Through this process, you can fully connect with the powerful forces of the universe and embrace the spiritual practices of religion.

The Role of the House

In the rich and vibrant tapestry of Louisiana Voodoo, practitioners are not simply lone individuals but are often part of a larger community called a "house." These houses are spiritual families that provide their members guidance, support, and protection. Practitioners are grouped into houses based on a shared spiritual lineage or tradition. Each house has its own unique practices, rituals, and beliefs, which have been passed down through generations of Voodoo practitioners. These houses often have a patriarch or matriarch, who is considered the spiritual leader and provides guidance to the members.

You stand to gain a lot when you're part of a house because it provides a sense of community and belonging and allows for deeper spiritual growth and development. Members of a house can learn from each other, share experiences, and support each other through the ups and downs of life. But being part of a house is not simply about socializing or having a sense of belonging. It is also a serious commitment to the practice of Voodoo. Houses are responsible for ensuring that their members follow correct protocol and conduct their spiritual work responsibly and respectfully. The role of a house is to provide a safe and supportive environment for its members to practice Voodoo and to guide them on their spiritual journeys. It is a place of learning and growth where practitioners can develop their abilities and gain a deeper understanding of the mysteries of the universe.

Becoming a Priestess or Priest

Voodoo is a way of life, a path to enlightenment, and a call to the divine. To answer the call of the spirits and become a houngan or mambo is not a decision to be taken lightly. It requires a deep commitment to faith, a willingness to learn, and a surrender to the mysteries of the universe. The path is not easy, but it is rewarding for those called to it. The process of becoming a houngan or mambo takes time and dedication. It is not something that can be rushed, nor can it be undertaken lightly. It requires a period of study, reflection, and contemplation under the guidance of an experienced priest or priestess.

Aspiring houngans and mambos must undergo a series of initiations, each one bringing them closer to the divine. These initiations are complex and highly ritualistic, with each step requiring the mastery of a new set of skills and knowledge. Through the initiations, the houngan or mambo becomes more deeply connected to the spirits and more capable of harnessing their power. The journey to becoming a houngan or mambo cannot be taken alone. It requires the support of a community, a house, of fellow practitioners who can guide and mentor the aspirant on their path.

These houses are not just social clubs but deeply spiritual organizations, each with its own traditions, practices, and secrets.

The role of a house is to provide a home for the practitioner, a place to develop their skills, to learn from others, and to be supported on their journey. The benefits of being in a house are many, including access to resources, protection from negative energy, and guidance from experienced practitioners. Being called to become a houngan or mambo is not a decision that is made lightly. It is a calling from the spirits, a path to enlightenment, and a way of life. For those who are called to it, the journey is difficult, but it is also one of the most rewarding and fulfilling paths one can undertake.

Mental Preparation

The following are essential tips to help you mentally prepare to practice Voodoo.

Spend time in nature: Take time to connect with nature and observe its cycles. Pay attention to the plants, animals, and elements around you. Nature is an essential element of Louisiana Voodoo, a religion that is deeply connected to the natural world. Practitioners of Voodoo believe that all things in nature, from the trees to the animals, are filled with spiritual energy that can be harnessed and channeled for magical purposes. Time outside allows you to connect with this energy and develop a deeper understanding of the natural cycles central to Voodoo practice.

When you spend time in nature, you can learn to recognize the signs of the changing seasons, the phases of the moon, and the rhythms of the tides. You can observe the behavior of animals and birds and learn to read the messages they may be trying to convey. By immersing yourself in the natural world, you can begin to attune yourself to the flow of energy that connects all living things and develop a greater sense of harmony and balance in your life.

For a Voodoo practitioner, this connection to the natural world is essential, as it provides a foundation for their magical work. By learning to work with the energy of the natural world, practitioners of Voodoo can harness this energy to create positive change in their lives and in the lives of those around them. So, take time to connect with nature, observe its cycles, and learn its secrets. In doing so, you will be preparing yourself to enter into the rich and complex world of Louisiana Voodoo.

Practice mindfulness: Practice being present in the moment, observing your thoughts without judgment. By cultivating mindfulness, you can develop a deeper connection with the spirits and the natural world.

Meditation is a great way to develop this important skill - a crucial element of the spiritual journey, allowing you to observe your thoughts and become aware of your surroundings. Through meditation, you can quiet your mind and focus on your breath, allowing you to be fully present in every waking moment.

This awareness allows you to connect with the Loa and the energy around you, opening the way for deeper spiritual experiences.

The following are exercises you can do to raise your vibration and get you in the right space mentally and energetically to practice Voodoo:

Candle-gazing Meditation

1. Find a quiet place to sit and light a candle. Make sure there's nothing around it that could catch fire.
2. Begin to focus on the flame, letting your eyes become fixated on it.
3. Allow your breathing to become deep and slow, and try to keep your focus on the flame.
4. As thoughts arise, acknowledge them, then return your focus to the flame.
5. Try to stay in this meditative state for at least 5-10 minutes.

Loving-Kindness Meditation

1. Find a quiet and comfortable place to sit or lie down.
2. Start by focusing on your breath, taking deep breaths in through your nose and out through your slightly parted lips.
3. Once you've found a calm and centered state, focus on the people you care about in your life.
4. Envision sending them positive energy and love, picturing it as a bright light radiating from your heart center.
5. Expand the circle of people you're sending love to, including those you may have difficult relationships with or even people you don't know well.
6. Finish the meditation by bringing the focus back to yourself, envisioning the same loving energy radiating from within you.

Read and study: Learn as much as possible about Voodoo's history, traditions, and practices. This can help you gain a deeper understanding and appreciation for the religion. To become a Voodooist, you must first immerse yourself in the rich history, traditions, and practices of the religion. Reading and studying can help you gain a deeper understanding and appreciation for Voodoo and provide a foundation for your own practice.

By learning about the origins and evolution of Voodoo, the beliefs and customs, the symbolism and rituals, you can begin to see the beauty and complexity of this ancient religion. Studying Voodoo can also help you understand the roles and responsibilities of a practitioner and how to approach the Loa with respect and humility. By reading about the experiences of other Voodoo practitioners, you can gain insight into the challenges and rewards of this path and learn from the wisdom of those who have gone before you. Remember, knowledge is power, and by arming yourself with knowledge about Voodoo, you can prepare yourself mentally and spiritually for the practice. With an open mind and a willing spirit, you can learn and grow in the ways of the Loa.

Connect with your ancestors: Honor your ancestors and learn about your family history. This can help you feel more grounded and connected to your roots. Connecting with your ancestors is crucial in preparing yourself to practice Voodoo. Ancestral veneration is an integral part of Voodoo, and the religion emphasizes maintaining a strong connection with one's lineage. By learning about your family history and honoring your ancestors, you gain a deeper understanding of your personal history and tap into the spiritual power believed to flow from one's ancestors. In Voodoo, the spirits of the dead are believed to profoundly influence the living. Practitioners who neglect to connect with their ancestors risk being cut off from this source of spiritual power. By tending to and improving relationships with your ancestors, you establish a foundation of respect and reverence that can help you navigate the complex spiritual landscape of Voodoo with grace and sensitivity.

Cultivate intuition: Practice trusting your gut instincts and intuition. You can start by paying attention to your body and noticing how it responds to different situations. Fostering your intuition is a critical component of preparing for the practice of Voodoo. Voodoo is a religion that values intuition, instinct, and spiritual discernment. When you learn to trust your intuition, you are more in tune with the energy and spirit around you. This awareness can help in your interactions with the Loa, your ancestors, and the world around you. By paying attention to your body, you can begin to recognize the signs and signals it gives you. Your gut instincts may alert you to situations that feel off or dangerous or guide you toward people and experiences that will be positive and uplifting. This practice of listening to your body and intuition can help you develop a deeper sense of trust in yourself and your instincts, which can be very beneficial in the practice of Voodoo.

In Voodoo, the Loa is believed to communicate with you through your intuition and spiritual senses. By developing your intuition, you may be better able to discern the messages and guidance the Loa send you. By strengthening your intuition and practicing spiritual discernment, you will be better equipped to navigate the Voodoo world and connect with its energies and entities.

The following are exercises that will help you with your intuition:

Body Scan Exercise

1. Find a quiet place to sit or lie down and close your eyes.
2. Take a few deep breaths and allow your body to relax. Breathe in through your nostrils and out through your slightly parted lips.
3. Starting at the top of your head, focus on each part of your body, one at a time, slowly moving down to your toes.
4. Notice any sensations, tension, or discomfort you feel in each area and observe them without judgment.
5. Allow yourself to feel any emotions or memories that may come up during the scan.
6. Now, allow that part of your body to relax. You can imagine it's made of cement, and it sinks deeper and deeper into relaxation, heavier with each breath.
7. After completing the scan, take a few deep breaths and slowly open your eyes.

Intuitive Journaling

1. Set aside time each day to sit and write in a journal.
2. Start by asking yourself a question or setting an intention for the session.

3. Write down any thoughts or feelings that come to mind without judgment or analysis.
4. Pay attention to any recurring themes or patterns in your writing.
5. After finishing your writing, take a few deep breaths and reflect on what you wrote.

Intuitive Decision-making

1. When faced with a decision, take a moment to pause and take a few deep breaths.
2. Tune in to your body and notice any physical sensations that arise.
3. Ask yourself how each option makes you feel, both emotionally and physically.
4. Pay attention to any intuitive nudges or insights that come up.
5. Make a decision based on what feels most aligned with your intuition rather than overthinking or analyzing.

You must understand that intuition is like a muscle. "Use it or lose it." You need to give it time to get stronger, and you must be consistent with the exercises to get better at reading your gut.

Recommended Reading

There are many books you could read to help you along your journey. Here is a list of five of the best ones available:

- *"Mama Lola: A Vodou Priestess in Brooklyn"* by Karen McCarthy Brown — This book is a personal account of the life and practice of a Haitian Vodou priestess, Mama Lola, who has been practicing for over 40 years. It provides an in-depth look at the day-to-day activities of a Vodou practitioner and includes an exploration of the religion's history, traditions, and beliefs.
- *"The New Orleans Voodoo Handbook"* by Kenaz Filan — This book includes information on the history, beliefs, and practices of Louisiana Voodoo.
- *"Voodoo in New Orleans"* by Robert Tallant — This book explores the history of Voodoo in New Orleans and includes information on the practice of Louisiana Voodoo.
- *"The Magic of Marie Laveau: Embracing the Spiritual Legacy of the Voodoo Queen of New Orleans"* by Denise Alvarado — This

book is a comprehensive guide to the practice of Louisiana Voodoo and includes information on the life and legacy of the famous Voodoo queen, Marie Laveau.

- *"The Rootworker's Guide to Healing and Wellness"* by Stephanie Rose Bird — This book includes information on the practice of rootwork, which is closely related to Louisiana Voodoo, and provides guidance on how to use herbs, roots, and other natural remedies for healing.

Please note that these recommendations are just a starting point and that many other books are available on Voodoo. As always, it is important to approach any new spiritual practice with an open mind and a spirit of inquiry and to do your own research to find the most helpful resources. You should educate yourself because Voodoo is a sacred religion. You can't just jump into it or do rituals just because you feel like it! Resist the temptation to play things by ear, and please don't just fool around with invoking spirits; instead, do the right thing by seeking to be formally initiated and respect this way of life.

If you want to learn more about how important spirits and ancestors are to the practice of Louisiana Voodoo and you're curious about how to energetically cleanse your home and keep it protected and safe, you're definitely going to want to keep reading.

Chapter Three: Ingredients and Materials You Might Need

The materials used in Voodoo spells are not merely physical ingredients but rather bear great spiritual significance. The practitioner needs to understand the significance of these materials and the roles they play in Voodoo rituals. Each material carries its own unique energy and spiritual symbolism, and the proper understanding of these elements is necessary for the successful practice of Louisiana Voodoo.

Herbs and roots, candles, and oils are the three primary materials used in Voodoo spells; each carries its own spiritual significance. Only by taking the time to understand the spiritual meanings of these materials can one properly harness their power and incorporate them into their rituals. By studying the meanings and uses of these materials, one can learn to create their own spells that align with their unique needs and intentions. Understanding the materials and their spiritual meanings is crucial for the successful practice of Louisiana Voodoo and for cultivating a deeper understanding of the religion as a whole.

Herbs and Roots

Herbs and roots play a vital role in Louisiana Voodoo. They are used in spells to harness the power of nature and work in tandem with the universe's energies. Regarding Voodoo, every plant and root has its own spiritual meaning, role, and usage in spells. One of the most essential aspects of working with herbs and roots in Voodoo is understanding their properties and their energies. It is said that every herb and root has its unique vibration, and when used in spells, it can help enhance the desired outcome. The following is a list of 59 herbs and roots, along with their spiritual meanings, roles, and usage in spells:

Herbs and roots are essential to voodoo practices.[17]

1. Angelica Root: used for protection, uncrossing, and luck in gambling spells.
2. Bay Leaf: used for protection and purification.
3. Black Cohosh: used for protection and cleansing.
4. Black Salt: used for protection and banishing.
5. Bladderwrack: used for protection and enhancing psychic powers.
6. Blessed Thistle: used for protection and purification.
7. Blue Cohosh: used for protection and enhancing psychic powers.
8. Boneset: used for protection and healing.
9. Calamus Root: used for commanding and controlling spells.
10. Camphor: used for purification and protection.
11. Catnip: used for love and luck spells.
12. Cedar: used for purification and protection.
13. Cinnamon: used for success, protection, and money spells.

14. Clove: used for protection and banishing spells.
15. Comfrey: used for protection and healing spells.
16. Copal: used for purification and cleansing.
17. Damiana: used for love and lust spells.
18. Dandelion: used for divination and calling spirits.
19. Devil's Shoestring: used for protection and luck spells.
20. Dragon's Blood: used for protection and purification.
21. Eucalyptus: used for healing and purification.
22. Fennel: Used for purification and protection.
23. Frankincense: used for purification and cleansing.
24. Five Finger Grass: used for attracting success and opportunities.
25. Galangal: used for uncrossing and protection.
26. Ginger: used for love and money spells.
27. Hawthorn: used for protection and banishing spells.
28. Hyssop: used for purification and protection.
29. Jasmine: used for love and psychic enhancement.
30. Juniper: used for protection and banishing spells.
31. Kava Kava: used for protection and psychic enhancement.
32. Lavender: used for love, purification, and healing.
33. Lemon Balm: used for love and happiness spells.
34. Lemon Grass: used for psychic enhancement and purification.
35. Licorice Root: used for commanding and controlling spells.
36. Lucky Hand Root: used for good luck.
37. Mandrake Root: used for protection and increasing personal power.
38. Mugwort: used for divination and enhancing psychic powers.
39. Mullein: used for protection and banishing spells.
40. Myrrh: used for purification and protection.
41. Nettle: used for protection and uncrossing spells.
42. Olive: used for protection and peace spells.
43. Orange Peel: used for love spells.
44. Patchouli: used for love and money spells.

45. Peppermint: used for purification and healing.
46. Pine: used for purification and protection.
47. Red Clover: used for love and money spells.
48. Rose: used for love and protection.
49. Rue: used for protection and uncrossing spells.
50. Sage: used for purification and protection.
51. Sandalwood: used for purification and protection.
52. Sweetgrass: used for purification.
53. Wormwood: spiritual grounding, protection, psychic abilities, divination
54. Yarrow: courage, love, psychic abilities, protection, exorcism
55. Yellow Dock: healing, money, fertility, attraction, success
56. Yerba Santa: purification, protection, spiritual growth, psychic abilities.
57. Ylang Ylang: love, romance, sensuality, calming, relaxation.
58. Zedoary: money, luck, protection, divination, love.
59. Zinnia: love, friendship, abundance, courage, happiness.

Candles

Candles play a vital role in Voodoo spells, as they are used to focus and direct energy towards a specific goal or intention. Different colors of candles have different meanings and are associated with specific purposes. In Voodoo, the color of the candle used in a spell is often chosen based on the desired outcome or intention of the practitioner. When choosing a candle for a spell, it is important to consider its color, size, and shape. Some practitioners prefer to use plain, unscented candles. In contrast, others prefer scented candles with specific aromas corresponding to the intention of the spell.

Different candles of varying colors symbolize intentions in voodoo rituals.[18]

Now let's talk about candle colors. The use of colors in Voodoo is based on the belief that each color represents a specific energy or intention. The origins of this practice are not entirely clear, as it is a part of the oral tradition passed down through generations of practitioners. However, it is believed that the use of colors in Voodoo can be traced back to West African spiritual practices. In Voodoo, each color is associated with certain attributes and energies. For example, red is often associated with passion, love, and courage, while black is associated with protection and banishing negative energies. Green is often associated with money, abundance, and prosperity, while white is associated with purity, peace, and healing.

The practice of using colors in Voodoo spells and rituals is based on the idea that like attracts like. By using candles, fabrics, or other materials of a certain color, practitioners can draw in the energy or intention associated with that color. For example, if someone wanted to attract love, they might use a red candle to represent the passion and energy of love. Remember that when you use colors in Voodoo, you're enhancing and directing the energy of your spell or ritual. Practitioners can create a powerful and effective spell or ritual by choosing the right color and understanding its associated energies and intentions. You can also blend colors, depending on what it is you want to accomplish. Here is a list of recommended candles and their spiritual meanings, roles, and usage in spells:

1. Red candle: used in love spells, passion spells, strength spells, and courage spells.
2. Pink candle: used in friendship spells, romance spells, and emotional healing spells.
3. Orange candle: used in creativity spells, success spells, and confidence spells.
4. Yellow candle: used in communication spells, clarity spells, and inspiration spells.
5. Green candle: used in fertility spells, growth spells, abundance spells, and financial success spells.
6. Blue candle: used in healing spells, peace spells, and tranquility spells
7. Purple candle: used in psychic ability spells, spirituality spells, and transformation spells.
8. White candle: used in purification spells, protection spells, and spiritual enlightenment spells.
9. Black candle: used in banishing negativity spells, breaking hexes spells, and protection spells.

When using candles in Voodoo spells, it is important to light them with intention, focusing your energy and attention on the desired outcome. Some practitioners prefer to anoint their candles with oils, carve symbols or words into them, or use them in conjunction with other materials such as crystals, herbs, or talismans to enhance the effectiveness of the spell.

Special Candles

Other kinds of special candles are used in Voodoo beyond traditional taper candles. Here are a few examples:

1. **Seven-day candles:** These are larger candles that are meant to burn continuously for seven days. They are often used in longer spells or rituals and can be inscribed with specific symbols or words.
2. **Figure candles:** These candles are shaped like people or animals and can be used to represent a specific individual or to draw upon the spiritual qualities of that person or animal. For example, a black cat candle could be used for protection or luck, while a red human-shaped candle could be used for love spells.

3. **Reversible candles:** These are candles that are black on one end and red on the other and are used in spells to reverse negativity or harm back onto the person who sent it.
4. **Double-action candles:** These are candles that have two colors, typically black on one end and another color (such as green or red) on the other. They are used to both remove negative energy and bring in positive energy.
5. **Jumbo candles:** These are large candles that come in a variety of shapes and colors. They can be used in place of multiple candles or to create a stronger, more intense flame.
6. **Skull candles:** These are molded in the shape of a human skull. They are used in spells related to communication with the dead and for spells related to mental powers and influencing others.
7. **Black cat candles:** These are candles shaped like a black cat. They are used in spells related to luck, protection, and even for breaking curses or hexes.
8. **Devil candles**: These are molded in the shape of a devil or a demon. They are used in spells related to banishing negative energies or entities.

Oils

The use of oils in New Orleans Voodoo is based on the belief that they possess spiritual and magical properties that can be harnessed to influence specific aspects of life. The roots of this practice can be traced back to the early African spiritual practices which formed the foundation of Voodoo. Many plants and herbs have been used for centuries for their medicinal and magical properties, and the essential oils extracted from these plants are believed to have similar properties.

In New Orleans Voodoo, oils are often used as part of spellwork, an important aspect of the tradition. Each oil is believed to have a specific spiritual meaning and can be used for various purposes, from attracting love and wealth to protection and banishing negative energies. When used with candles, herbs, and other ritual tools, oils are believed to enhance the spell's effectiveness.

The exact origins of the use of oils in Voodoo are unclear, but it is believed to have been a common practice among many African and Afro-Caribbean spiritual traditions. Some believe that the use of oils may have been influenced by ancient Egyptian and other Middle Eastern cultures, which also used essential oils in religious ceremonies and as part of healing practices. Oils are absolutely important when it comes to spellwork. You see, oils are used in many different ways in the practice of Voodoo, from anointing candles and other objects to dressing oneself for a ritual. Each oil has its own unique spiritual meaning, role, and usage in spells, and knowing which oil to use for a particular purpose is key to success in Voodoo. Now, here are 54 of the recommended oils in Louisiana Voodoo, along with their spiritual meanings, roles, and usage in spells:

- Almond oil: prosperity, fertility, and wisdom
- Basil oil: purification, protection, and prosperity
- Bayberry oil: prosperity, success, and protection
- Bay leaf oil: protection, purification, and psychic abilities
- Benzoin oil: purification, protection, and prosperity
- Bergamot oil: money, success, and mental clarity
- Black pepper oil: protection, purification, and energy
- Camphor oil: purification and protection
- Caraway oil: protection, purification, and mental clarity
- Cardamom oil: love, sensuality, and mental clarity
- Cedarwood oil: purification, protection, and healing
- Chamomile oil: relaxation, purification, and psychic abilities
- Cinnamon oil: love, success, and power
- Citronella oil: repelling negative energy and insects
- Clove oil: protection, love, and wealth
- Coconut oil: purification and protection
- Cypress oil: protection, purification, and healing
- Dragon's Blood oil: protection and banishing negative energy
- Eucalyptus oil: healing, purification, and protection
- Frankincense oil: spiritual purification, protection, and healing
- Gardenia oil: love, peace, and protection
- Fennel oil: purification, protection, and prosperity

- Geranium oil: love, sensuality, and psychic abilities
- Ginger oil: love and prosperity
- Grapefruit oil: energy and protection
- Jasmine oil: love, spiritual growth, and psychic abilities
- Juniper oil: protection, purification, and healing
- Lavender oil: relaxation, peace, and healing
- Lemon oil: purification, protection, and love
- Lemongrass oil: purification, protection, and psychic abilities
- Lime oil: purification, love, and healing
- Lotus oil: spiritual growth, enlightenment, and purity
- Magnolia oil: love, attraction, and purity
- Mint oil: healing, purification, and prosperity
- Musk oil: sensuality, attraction, and grounding
- Myrrh oil: purification, protection, and healing
- Neroli oil: love, relaxation, and purification
- Nutmeg oil: luck, prosperity, and clarity
- Orange oil: love, purification, and energy
- Orris root oil: divination, psychic abilities, and protection
- Patchouli oil: love, prosperity, and grounding
- Peppermint oil: purification, protection, and mental clarity
- Pine oil: purification, protection, and healing
- Rose oil: love, beauty, and psychic abilities
- Rosemary oil: protection, purification, and mental clarity
- Sandalwood oil: purification, protection, and healing
- Spearmint oil: healing, purification, and protection
- Sweetgrass oil: purification, protection, and spiritual growth
- Tea tree oil: purification, protection, and healing
- Thyme oil: courage, purification, and protection
- Vanilla oil: love, sensuality, and passion
- Vetiver oil: grounding, protection, and sensuality

- Yarrow oil: protection, healing, and psychic abilities
- Ylang-ylang oil: love, sensuality, and relaxation

Safety Matters!

It is of utmost importance to note that some of the herbs and oils used in Voodoo practices can be quite dangerous if ingested or used improperly. Anyone wishing to engage in such practices must do so cautiously and carefully. For example, the ingestion of certain herbs can lead to serious health issues; even contact with certain oils can result in skin irritation or allergic reactions. Additionally, ensuring that any items used in Voodoo spells do not harm the environment is vital. So, once more, when it comes to using herbs and oils in Voodoo practices, you must exercise great care, respect, and responsibility.

It is important to note that pregnant women should be cautious when using any type of oil, especially during the first trimester. Oils that should be avoided during pregnancy include basil, birch, camphor, cinnamon, clary sage, clove, fennel, hyssop, juniper, marjoram, myrrh, peppermint, rosemary, sage, and thyme. Some oils are more likely to cause allergic reactions than others. These include cinnamon, clove, lemongrass, and tea tree oils. It is always recommended to perform a patch test before using any new oil or product on the skin.

Individuals with certain medical conditions should avoid using certain oils. For example, those with high blood pressure should avoid using stimulating oils such as rosemary and peppermint, while individuals with epilepsy should avoid using stimulating oils such as rosemary, peppermint, and eucalyptus. People with asthma should avoid using oils that may trigger an attack, such as eucalyptus and peppermint.

It is also important to note that some oils can be toxic to animals and plants. Oils such as tea tree, cinnamon, and citrus oils can be toxic to cats and dogs. When using oils around pets, it is important to use them in a well-ventilated area and ensure that pets cannot ingest or come into contact with them. Additionally, some oils can be harmful to plants. For example, peppermint oil can be toxic to certain plants and may even kill them. When using oils around plants, it is important to research their effects beforehand and to use caution when applying oils near plants.

Now, you're probably dying to get to know more about the Creator and his helper spirits. In the next chapter, you'll get all your burning questions answered and then some.

Chapter Four: Bondye and the Loa Pantheon

You cannot claim to practice Voodoo without knowing everything there is to know about Bondye, or the Supreme Creator, as well as the Loa (or Lwa). These are the most important aspects of Voodoo.

Bondye is the supreme creator of the universe.[19]

Voodoo Gods, Catholic Saints

From 1501, Africans were enslaved and taken to the Caribbean colonies to be put to work on sugar plantations and mines. It would remain so until

1821 – when Spain would finally declare the slave trade illegal. By 1860, there were about 350,000 enslaved people in Cuba. These people comprised many Yoruba people from Nigeria, and they were from Ijebu, Ife, Kesu, and Egba, among other Yoruba regions. Now, you can find these same people in Togo and Benin, too. The Yorubas who arrived were natural farmers. Their culture had a societal structure made up of different kingdoms.

One thing to note about Yoruba culture is that it has a very rich mythology. Take the Yoruba pantheon, for instance. It's a rather broad one, made up of divine beings. Each one is known as an Orisa (pronounced o-ri-sha). Sometimes, the word is spelled "Orisha." Among them are Sango (pronounced shaw-ngo), Oyo (pronounced aw-yaw), Yemoja, Egba, Obatala, Ogun, etc. These beings are the ones who keep the Yoruba people safe. When the enslaved Africans were coerced into leaving their lands for Brazil, Haiti, Cuba, and Santo Domingo, they had to find creative ways to continue to practice their religion. This led to Voodoo's syncretism with Roman Catholicism, the latter being the religion of the colonial masters.

Syncretism is simply the process of combining different religious views or ideologies to fit each other. It's about merging different practices, theologically speaking, so that there's some form of unity, making it possible for one to practice different religions without dealing with the cognitive dissonance that inevitably arises from trying to follow two distinctly different ways of life. So, there was a blend of Voodoo with Roman Catholicism. You can also find elements of Freemasonry as well.

The Black Codes, also known as the Code Noir, were implemented during the French and Spanish colonization of New Orleans. This was in 1724. The codes were meant to cover all things related to the enslaved people's affairs. The code also stipulated that they were not permitted to practice their religions out in the open. It also stipulated that all enslavers had to convert the enslaved people to Christianity no later than eight days after they got to the colony. They were to be taught Roman Catholic beliefs and had to be baptized as well. So as the enslaved people were taught about Catholicism, they found ways to incorporate their traditional African beliefs with what they were learning.

Sometimes, the enslavers were a little "kinder" because of the festivities of holidays like Easter and Christmas. They would let the enslaved people have liberty, if only for a while. The people were still colonized but would be allowed some time off to spend the holidays as they liked. They also had some free time on Sunday afternoons. The enslaved people took advantage of their freedom — which should have been rightfully theirs anyway — to practice their religions with others. Sunday afternoons, they would all meet up in Congo Square, an area designated by the rules in New Orleans for the African people to get together. There, they would create their own customs and traditions.

The people found a way to connect their deities or Loa with the Roman Catholic saints. For instance, in Saint Peter, they saw Papa Legba since he is known as the one who unlocks the spirit realm to grant access to it, and Saint Peter is usually painted or drawn with keys in hand. In the Mater Dolorosa, they found Ezili Freda, a Loa who loves everything to do with luxury and love. In Saint Patrick, the Voodooists found Damballa, a snake. The saint is usually shown with snakes. Sometimes they consider Damballa to be Moses since he was the one whose staff became a snake that swallowed all the other snakes of the Egyptian priests when God sent him to free the Israelites. Cosmos and Damian were originally physicians of Arab origin, twin brothers who would eventually become Christian martyrs. In them, the Africans saw the Marasa, who are sacred twin Loas.

Bondye

Voodoo is a practice centered on the belief in a creator known as Bondye. Etymologically, the name Bondye is from the French Bon Dieu, meaning "Good God." This is the uncreated Creator who is in charge of all things. Some refer to this creator as Gran Met, meaning the Great Master. In terms of ideology, this God is almost the same as the Christian concept of God. However, when it comes to Voodoo, no one is to approach Bondye directly because that would be disrespectful and an exercise in futility.

The way to approach Bondye is through the Lwa (or Loa), who represent the different expressions of the Creator's power. Approaching Bondye directly is pointless because this being is beyond your comprehension since you're human, and he's so much more. So, the only way to get through to him and receive from him is through the Loa. This is why Voodooists turn their attention to these beings instead and why you'll never hear anyone claim that *Bondye himself* has possessed them. Does this mean Bondye doesn't care about human affairs? Of course not. You must understand that everything is part of Bondye's plan — even when it doesn't seem that way.

Every Voodooist knows that there's not a single person or thing that isn't connected to the Gran Met. Therefore, Bondye must be acknowledged and honored using the correct methods and rites at all ceremonies. This being is shrouded in mystery and is beyond human comprehension. He is the Unknowable who knows all, the one who keeps the wheel of life spinning in perpetuity. Some people may erroneously assume that because Bondye is literally the "Good God," there is some equal and opposing force that one might call "Mal Dieu" or the "Bad God." That is not the case at all.

Naturally, this would cause some confusion for those who are used to assuming that all things in religion require duality. And this should, also naturally, cause you to wonder what the concepts of good and bad are in Bondye's eyes and in the eyes of the true Voodooist. The thing to understand is that it's not about good and bad but about the extent of the demonstration of Bondye's presence in your life. This demonstration comes down to the choices you make. So, doing things that bode well for you financially, physically, and in any other aspect of life is a good thing. When you do things that take away from that well-being, this would be considered as bad.

There's not a single person not made in the image of Bondye. There's nothing and no one who doesn't have Bondye's essence flowing through them. He crafted humanity using only clay and water, working with the very elements he used to create the world. Voodooists understand that they come from the earth and that it's no coincidence that when humans pass away, they return to the earth. Since all people are made of the same stuff that the earth is, it is a deeply rooted belief in Voodoo that there's not a thing that can work against you, even when it seems that way, since humans are all made of the same stuff.

The Loa Pantheon

The Loa or Lwa are divided into various pantheons, also known as nanchons (meaning "nations") or families. Each of these has its own requirements, methodologies, and ethos regarding rites and ceremonies. It is said there are at least seventeen nanchons, but they're not all very popular or known, and some of them have been assimilated into the major ones. For instance, pantheons like the Wangol and Nago, also known as the Ibo and Kongo, are now a part of the Petro pantheon. The major pantheons are:

1. The Rada Loa
2. The Petro Loa
3. The Gede Loa

You may have heard someone claim that the Petro Loa are bad and that the Rada are the good guys. That person is sadly misinformed. Regarding the Loa, you cannot apply regular ethics to them and their magic. To be clear, there was once a period when the Petro was viewed as being connected to evil magic only, while the Rada was deemed as good. This led to the misconception that the Petro Loa are dangerous destroyers best left alone and that the Rada are very forgiving and lenient.

The truth of the matter is that Petro is capable of goodness and has demonstrated this time and time again. Also, as peaceful and sweet as the Rada Loa are, their revenge can be swift and ruthless if you cross them. You could ask devotees who fail to perform their religious obligations, and they'll tell you as much. So, avoid the trap of using basic ideas of morality to define the Loa pantheons. This doesn't mean you should assume Voodoo is a way of life free from morality and that you now have the license to be a terrible person. As a Voodooist, you are clear about right and wrong, and you also understand that, at the end of the day, it's all about your service to the Loa and ultimately to Bondye, who is the one who maintains the world as you know it.

The Rada Loa Pantheon

The etymological root of Rada is Arada, a Dahomien kingdom that existed during the colonization of Haiti. The Rada Loa are sometimes called the Gentle Ones because they're cool-headed and sweet. Before taking any action, they must carefully consider all the facts of the situation. For this reason, you can be sure that the judgment they deliver is just and deserved. They are particular about maintaining balance and harmony in all things.

The great thing about the Rada pantheon is that you can always depend on them. They love to be as connected to their loyal followers as possible, and they love the idea of family. You can tell from their names how much familial connections mean to them. All the rituals involved in the adoration of these Loa come from the Arada kingdom. One of the peculiar things about these beings is that their color is white, so it's not unusual to notice white cloths and other white things on altars dedicated to them. Some of the Rada Loa include, but aren't limited to:

- Papa Legba, who keeps the door and the gate.
- Ounto, the Loa of the drums.
- Marassa, the divine twins.
- Damballa Wedo, the spirit of peace and tranquility, and the Serpent Father
- Sobo, who brings prosperity
- La Sirene, the seductress who rules the sea
- Granne Halouba, the wise woman
- Erzilie Freda, the sweet Queen of beauty, luxury, and wealth.
- Bossou, the powerful bull
- Klemezin, the one who brings enlightenment
- Lovana, the one who removes obstacles

The Petro Loa Pantheon

The word "Petro" is said to come from Dom Pedro, the one who was at the helm of the 18th-century maroon rebellion. The spirits in this pantheon can also be collectively referred to as compete. These are the hot-headed spirits, and their ways are rather volatile. Everything about them is aggressive, but this is not necessarily bad. There is such a thing as positive aggression, you know. When they take action, there's an undeniable force about them. Regarding altars, it's best to have theirs separate from the Rada Loa's in the *ounfo* (meaning "temple"). You should also never invoke them at the same time as you invoke the Rada during your rituals and ceremonial rites.

Every Voodooist knows that the Petro Loa always come through dramatically, and for some reason, they're particularly good at making things happen regarding money. If you'll offer the Petro Loa anything, be prepared to give them coffee, hot peppers, alcohol, cigarettes, blood, and other things of that nature. If you ever witness a ceremony or ritual for these beings, you'll notice that the drumming is at a really rapid pace and feels very powerful, sometimes harsh. You'll see Voodooists with whips that they crack. Some blow whistles pretty loudly, and there's also exploding gunpowder. These Loa have red as their color, and in light of everything you've just read about them, it only makes sense. Some of the Petro Loa include but aren't limited to the following:

- Kalfou, the crossroads spirit
- Simbi Andeazo, the spirit of saltwater and freshwater, of the rain, and of baths
- Ti Jean Petro, the spirit of fire and revolution
- Gran Bwa, the tree spirit, the one who rules the night forest
- Simitye, he who brings change, the connection between Petro and Gede
- Ezili Danto, mother of Haiti
- Linglinsou, a violent spirit of vengeance

The Gede Loa Pantheon

Sometimes, Gede is spelled *Ghede* or *Guede*. These Loa are in charge of all matters concerning death and fertility. Their musical drumming and dancing style is known as *Banda*. Like the other Loa, they can and do possess the Voodooists around. When they do, they'll typically douse themselves in a mixture of 21 Scotch bonnet peppers and a raw sugarcane rum known as *clairin*. Sometimes they use goat peppers instead.

The Gede Loa is usually celebrated during a festival known as the Fet Gede, which happens on November 2nd each year. This is like All Souls' Day or the Festival of the Dead. Those who are devoted to these Loa will enjoy their generosity. If any good has been done for the people that has not been appreciated, they know that the Loa will avenge their lack of appreciation. These beings are very sensual. If you're not already familiar with their ways, you may find yourself appalled, but there's no reason to be. Irreverent beings, their dancing is a mimicry of sex. They're known for taking the dead to the next stage of life. The color of this pantheon is black. These are some of the Gede Loa:

- Papa Gede, the psychopomp
- Brav Gede, he who watches the graveyard
- Guede Nibo, the psychopomp and patron of those who passed on unnaturally
- Maman Brigitte, protector of gravestones
- Baron Criminel, the enforcer and first murderer

We'll look further into each pantheon in subsequent chapters, but for now, if you'd like to learn more about the Loa, you can always do some research.

Veves

In Voodoo, the devotees of Loas will occasionally ask the Loa to come and take over their bodies so that through them, they may communicate with others and interact with them. This isn't something that's just done anywhere, anytime. There are rituals with specific practices that must be followed to the letter. During rituals, you can expect to witness dancing, drumming, chanting, and other displays, especially when the possession has happened. During these rituals, veves become vital. These are special symbols that are connected to individual Loa. In the same way, every Loa has special dances, drum rhythms, colors, and so on, and they also have unique symbols that carry their energy. Usually, the veves are drawn on the sandy floor of the ritual space or on any powdery substance on the floor.

As the rituals carry on, the veves will serve as a platform of sorts where devotees can place their offerings to the Loa. It is important that the offerings made are energetically in resonance with the veves and the Loa that the devotees intend to invoke. Once the veve is drawn, libations are poured on it, and a candle is set in its center. To infuse life and energy into the veve, a devotee must ring a bell as everyone prays to the Loa. If there is ever a need to summon more than one Loa, all their veves must be drawn and linked, and special attention is given to the sort of powdery substance used for each of the Loa. Some like coffee powder, others prefer brick powder, and others prefer white powder.

While every Loa's veve is different (and with some Loa having more than one veve), some things remain constant with all of them. The veve acts as a lighthouse to draw all relevant ships to it. It is meant to draw the attention of the Loa, and not only that, but it also acts as an amplifier of the Loa's energy in that space. You may assume, therefore, that tattooing yourself with a Loa's veve would be just the thing to do to keep their presence with you always, or that you can just put it up wherever you want to in your home without much thought, but that's not the case.

Please don't tattoo yourself with a veve. The odds are, the Loa may choose to ignore you when you need them — and that's the best-case scenario. The worst thing that could happen due to you disrespecting the veves like that is you may upset the Petro spirits, and you already know that you don't want to be on their bad side. When using a veve, your intent must be clear and sincere. Again, Voodoo is a way of life, not an "aesthetic" to be shown off. Please treat it accordingly.

Now, it's time to look at some of the powerful female Loa of Louisiana Voodoo.

Chapter Five: Major Female Loa

This chapter takes a look at the most important Loa of Louisiana Voodoo, who are females. To be clear, this chapter doesn't cover every single female Loa in existence, so you may want to do further research if you would like to learn about any that aren't mentioned here.

Maman Brigitte

Maman Brigitte is the Loa of death and cemeteries in Louisiana Voodoo. She is a fiery and powerful force to be reckoned with and has a personality reflecting her association with death and the afterlife.

Maman Brigitte is the Loa of death.[30]

In appearance, Maman Brigitte is often depicted as a tall, statuesque woman with dark skin and fiery red hair. She is said to be regal and fierce, with piercing eyes that can see into the souls of those who cross her path.

Her veve is a powerful symbol, featuring a heart above a triangle and other intricate lines and patterns. Other symbols include a skull, crossbones, snake, and coffin. These symbols represent her connection to death and the afterlife and her role as a powerful healer and protector.

Maman Brigitte is often syncretized with the Roman Catholic saint, St. Brigid, known for her healing powers and association with fire and light.

In terms of her correspondences, Maman Brigitte is associated with the color purple and hot peppers, rum, and tobacco. She is said to be particularly fond of the herb rue, which is used in many Voodoo rituals and spells.

Maman Brigitte is closely associated with the Gede family of Loa, known for their irreverent and bawdy personalities. She is said to have a close relationship with Baron Samedi, the Loa of death and resurrection. She is often called upon to help guide souls to the afterlife.

Bits of lore connected to Maman Brigitte often depict her as a strong-willed, fearless woman unafraid of death or the unknown. She is said to have a fierce temper and a no-nonsense attitude but also a deep compassion for those seeking her guidance.

Preferred offerings for Maman Brigitte include rum, hot peppers, tobacco, and items associated with death and the afterlife, such as black candles and images of skulls or cemeteries. Signs that she has received and accepted one's offering may include a feeling of warmth or a sudden change in the atmosphere.

Maman Brigitte is celebrated and honored in New Orleans during the annual Day of the Dead festival and other Voodoo ceremonies throughout the year. She is often called upon to help guide souls to the afterlife and to offer protection to those who seek her aid.

Ezili Freda

In the world of Voodoo, there is a Loa known for her beauty, her elegance, and her love for all things luxurious. This is Ezili Freda, the Loa of love, sensuality, and luxury. Ezili Freda is often depicted as a light-skinned, beautiful woman dressed in a flowing white gown and adorned with pearls and other fine jewelry. Her veve, or sacred symbol, is a heart-shaped design that is often drawn in pink, white, and blue powders. She is syncretized with the Catholic saints Our Lady of Lourdes and the Immaculate Conception.

Ezili Freda.

https://www.wallpaperflare.com/woman-female-girl-white-dress-wood-forest-sleep-walking-wallpaper-aotmf

As the Loa of love and sensuality, Ezili Freda is associated with pink, white, and gold. She is often offered champagne, pink roses, and sweets such as white cake, sugar, and honey. In terms of plants and herbs, she is associated with jasmine, ylang-ylang, and vanilla. Ezili Freda is known to be a very powerful and respected Loa in the Voodoo pantheon. She is often seen as a mother figure and is revered for her ability to bring people together in love and harmony. Her relationships with other Loa are complex, but she is often associated with her counterpart, the Loa of war and struggle, Ogou, who is her protector and champion.

This Loa has connections to other spirits that run deep. Her nature as a love goddess means that she has ties to other spirits who oversee affairs of the heart, such as Ezili Dantor and Legba. However, despite her gracious and tender personality, Ezili Freda is also known for her caprice and temperamental behavior, which can cause conflict with other Loa. She is known to be particularly at odds with her darker counterpart, Ezili Dantor, who represents the other side of love, including jealousy and revenge. Additionally, her demanding nature and high expectations can create tension with other Loa, particularly those who do not meet her standards.

Despite these conflicts, Ezili Freda remains one of the most beloved and revered Loa in the Voodoo pantheon due to her ability to bring happiness, abundance, and harmony to the lives of those who honor her. The lore surrounding Ezili Freda is rich and varied. She is often described as a passionate and loving Loa who will go to great lengths to help those who call upon her. She is also known for her vanity and materialism, which can make her a challenging Loa to work with. It is said that she requires the finest offerings and gifts and that she can be quite particular in her tastes.

To honor Ezili Freda, practitioners of Voodoo often hold lavish parties and celebrations in her honor. These celebrations are filled with music, dancing, and offerings of champagne and sweet treats. In New Orleans, she is often celebrated during Mardi Gras and the annual Voodoo Festival.

Ezili Dantor

Ezili Dantor, Haiti's warrior and protector goddess, is one of the most powerful Loas in the Voodoo pantheon. She is known as a fierce defender of women and children, and her legend is steeped in bravery and tragedy. Ezili Dantor is often depicted as a black woman with scars and wearing a blue and red scarf around her head. She is armed with a machete and can be seen with a child at her feet or on her hip, which represents her maternal and protective nature. Her veve, the symbol used to invoke her energy, is typically drawn with a heart and a sword.

Ezili Dantor.[21]

She is syncretized with the Catholic Saints, most often with the Black Madonna of Częstochowa, and is associated with the colors gold, green, red, and blue. Her offerings include rum, spicy food, and her favorite flower, the hibiscus. This Loa is known for her fiery and passionate nature, which makes her both a force to be reckoned with and a powerful protector. She is fiercely independent, and her independence is one of the main reasons she is so beloved by women. She is often associated with revolutionaries and is seen as an embodiment of the spirit of resistance.

Ezili Dantor has a complex relationship with her sister Loa, Ezili Freda. Although they are sisters, they have very different personalities and often clash with each other. Despite this, they are both associated with love and often invoked together to create a harmonious relationship. A powerful Loa, it is important that offerings to her are taken seriously. She is said to prefer offerings made in secret or in a private space, and those who make offerings to her must be pure of heart and intention. When she is pleased with an offering, it is said that she will protect and guide the person who made it.

Ezili Dantor is honored and celebrated in various ways throughout the year in New Orleans. One of the most popular celebrations is held on the day of Our Lady of Mount Carmel, July 26th. During this celebration, offerings are made to her, and her followers dance and sing in her honor. This Petro Loa is also honored during the Festival of the Dead and other Voodoo ceremonies.

Simbi

Simbi is a powerful Loa in Louisiana Voodoo, often associated with serpents and water. She is known to take on many forms but is most commonly depicted as a serpent with a woman's head or a woman with a serpent's tail. Her veve, a sacred symbol used in Voodoo rituals, features the image of a serpent with a wave-like pattern.

Simbi.[22]

In Haitian Vodou, Simbi is often syncretized with Saint Patrick, who is said to have driven the snakes out of Ireland. Simbi is also associated with the Catholic Saint John the Baptist and is sometimes called "Simbi St. Jean."

The colors most commonly associated with Simbi are green and blue, and her corresponding plants include water lilies, cattails, and snakeroot. She is said to have dominion over rivers, streams, and other bodies of water and is often called upon for help with fertility, healing, and divination matters.

Simbi is known to have interesting connections to several other Loa, as her role and abilities overlap with theirs. For example, she is sometimes associated with the Loa Agwe, who is also a water spirit. In some traditions, she is seen as Agwe's wife; in others, they are considered two aspects of the same Loa. Similarly, Simbi is sometimes associated with the Loa Damballah, a serpent spirit. In some traditions, she is seen as Damballah's wife; in others, they are considered two aspects of the same Loa.

Simbi is also often associated with Loa Ayida Wedo, who is Damballah's female counterpart. Ayida Wedo is also a water spirit and is often depicted as a rainbow. Simbi and Ayida Wedo are sometimes seen as opposing forces, with Simbi representing water's dark, dangerous aspects and Ayida Wedo representing water's peaceful, life-giving aspects. In other traditions, however, they are seen as complementary forces, with Simbi representing the power and strength of water and Ayida Wedo representing its beauty and grace.

She is also sometimes associated with Loa Ezili, a spirit of love and sexuality. In some traditions, Simbi is seen as Ezili's husband; in others, they are considered two aspects of the same Loa. This association may reflect the fact that in Voudou, water is often associated with emotions and relationships.

Simbi's lore is rich and varied, with stories depicting her as compassionate and vengeful. She is said to be a wise teacher and healer but can also be dangerous when crossed. In one legend, she transformed a man into a snake after he insulted her. In another, she is used her power to create a healing spring for a sick child.

Offerings to Simbi vary depending on the situation but can include offerings of water, herbs, and candles. She appears to enjoy offerings of tobacco and rum and is often depicted with a cigar in her mouth. Signs that Simbi has received and accepted an offering can include the flickering of candles or water movement. In New Orleans, Simbi is often celebrated as part of the annual St. John's Eve celebration on June 23rd. This festival is a time to honor the relationship between Simbi and St. John the Baptist and is marked by bonfires, dancing, and other rituals. Simbi is also sometimes invoked during Mardi Gras and other Voodoo ceremonies throughout the year.

Gran Ibo

Gran Ibo, or *Gran Yobo* or *Grannibo,* is a powerful and enigmatic Loa in the Voodoo pantheon. Considered the "Mother of Nature," she is associated with the forces of the Earth, particularly with the trees and the mountains. Her image is of an elderly woman with a powerful presence, often depicted wearing a headdress made of leaves or branches and carrying a staff made of wood or metal.

Gran Ibo is considered to be mother nature.[38]

The veve, or sacred symbol, of Gran Ibo, is a unique and intricate design that is often drawn on the ground with cornmeal or flour as a ritual invocation of her presence. The symbol features a central tree surrounded by several other elements, including a snake, a turtle, and a representation of the sun. Gran Ibo is syncretized with Saint Jerome, and her feast day is celebrated on September 30th. Her correspondences include green and brown colors, and her associated plants are oak, pine, and avocado.

As a Loa of nature and the wilderness, Gran Ibo is said to have close relationships with other earthy Loa, including Damballah, Simbi, and Agwe. She is also known for her ability to heal the sick and injured, particularly through the use of herbal remedies and spiritual cleansing. In Voodoo lore, Gran Ibo is often depicted as a powerful and wise figure who provides guidance and protection to those who seek her aid. She is known to be a strict but fair teacher, and those needing spiritual guidance often seek her wisdom.

To honor Gran Ibo, you can offer her candles, fruits, and flowers, particularly those associated with her, such as oak leaves and pine needles. Signs that she has accepted your offering may include the appearance of a snake or turtle or a sense of calm and balance in your surroundings. In New Orleans, Gran Ibo is celebrated as a vital force of nature, and her presence can be felt in the lush greenery of the city's many parks and gardens. She is often honored through public celebrations and rituals, particularly on her feast day. If you seek her wisdom and guidance, look to the natural world and allow her spirit to guide you on your journey.

Chapter Six: Major Male Loa

In this chapter, you will learn about the major male Loa in Louisiana Voodoo. Once more, please note that there's no way to cover every one of them in existence, so if there are some that you're interested in that aren't mentioned here, you should do some research. Having said that, it's time to check out the most accessible and popular male Loa.

Papa Legba

Papa Legba is the powerful gatekeeper and intermediary between the spirit and human worlds. In the realm of the Vodou, he is one of the most important and widely venerated Loa. He is often depicted as an elderly man but also as a young man with a limp. He is known for his smile, the kindness in his eyes, and the wisdom that emanates from his being. His image is often associated with the colors red and black. The veve, or ritual symbol, for Papa Legba, is a crossroads with a circle around it. He is considered the opener of the gates between the worlds.

This Loa is often syncretized with St. Peter in the Catholic religion, as both are gatekeepers. However, some also associate him with St. Lazarus or St. Anthony. He is closely associated with communication and language and is believed to be able to speak every human tongue. Some of the herbs associated with him include tobacco, coffee, and corn, while his corresponding colors include red and black.

As with most Loa, this one also has some fascinating ties to many of the others. He is often seen as the intermediary between the human and spiritual realms and is responsible for granting access to other spirits. In this role, he has developed intricate relationships with other Loa. For example, Papa Legba is often associated with the Loa Loco, who is the patron of healers and plants. Together, they are seen as the guardians of the crossroads and work together to maintain a balance between the worlds. Papa Legba also closely relates to Damballa, who represents the sky and creation. They work together to maintain balance in the natural world.

He also has a relationship with Ezili, particularly Loas Ezili Freda and Ezili Dantor. With Ezili Freda, they share an association with love and beauty and are often called upon together to bring blessings of fertility and prosperity. With Ezili Dantor, they share an association with motherhood and protection. They are often called upon together for help with familial issues. In addition, Papa Legba is connected to Baron Samedi, who is the lord of the dead. They are often seen as opposites, with Papa Legba representing life and light, while Baron Samedi represents death and darkness. Despite their differences, they are both seen as essential to maintaining the balance between life and death.

His role as the gatekeeper and intermediary between the worlds makes him integral to the Vodou tradition. He is often seen as the first and last Loa to be called upon during Vodou ceremonies, and all communication with the other Loa must pass through him.

Often depicted as playful and mischievous, he is also wise and powerful. He is said to protect children and have a great fondness for dancing and singing.

Offerings to Papa Legba can include rum, cigars, coffee, and candy. Some also offer keys, as he is known as the "key holder." Signs that he has received and accepted one's offering can include feeling his presence, such as hearing his voice or experiencing a sudden breeze. In New Orleans, Papa Legba is celebrated on the feast day of St. Anthony, which falls on June 13th. He is often honored with ritual offerings, dances, and ceremonies, as he is considered an important part of the local Vodou tradition.

Baron Samedi

Baron Samedi, the Loa of death, is a complex and fascinating figure in the Vodou tradition. He is often depicted as a skeleton in a black top hat, black coat, and dark glasses, with a cigar in his mouth and a bottle of rum in his hand. Despite his association with death, he is a beloved figure and brings joy and laughter to those who honor him.

His veve, a sacred symbol used in Vodou rituals, often features an image of a skull, crossed bones, and a top hat. His symbols also include a shovel, a black rooster, and a rattle made from human bones. In syncretic Catholicism, Baron Samedi is often identified with Saint Martin de Porres or Saint Expedite, but his true essence lies in the depths of the Vodou tradition. The color associated with Baron Samedi is black, representing death and the afterlife's mysteries. Plants and herbs associated with him include belladonna, tobacco, and wormwood, often used in rituals and offerings.

Baron Samedi is a member of the Ghede family of Loa, which is associated with death and fertility. He is often portrayed as the husband of Maman Brigitte, the Loa of death and cemeteries. He is also known for his close relationship with the Loa of healing and fertility, Ayizan, and the Loa of the crossroads, Papa Legba. Baron Samedi is known for his playful and mischievous personality. He is often depicted as a trickster, and his humor and wit are renowned among those who honor him. He is also known for his sexual prowess and is often seen as a symbol of fertility and virility.

Offerings to Baron Samedi typically include rum, cigars, and spicy foods. His offerings are often left at the entrance to cemeteries, which are his sacred spaces. Signs that he has accepted an offering may include the sound of laughter, the movement of objects, or the presence of the scent of rum or cigars. Baron Samedi is celebrated in New Orleans during the annual Vodou Festival and other Vodou ceremonies. He is also honored during the Day of the Dead, a celebration of the ancestors, which takes place in early November. The Baron is a powerful and enigmatic figure in the Vodou tradition. His association with death and the afterlife makes him both feared and revered, but his playful and humorous nature endears him to those who honor him.

Damballah

Damballah, the snake Loa of Haitian Vodou, is a powerful and revered deity who is often associated with creation, fertility, and the natural world. He is usually represented as a long, coiling serpent, often with a white or silver color and with a penchant for shedding its skin. Damballah is known to be a very old and wise Loa, often depicted as a great serpent in the sky, and is said to possess deep knowledge and wisdom about the mysteries of life and the universe.

The veve of Damballah is often portrayed as a serpent coiled around a pole, with symbols such as sunbursts, moon crescents, and stars surrounding it. His associated colors are white, silver, and pale blue, and he is linked to plants such as basil, thyme, and sage. Damballah's closest relation is his wife, Ayida Wedo, and the two are often depicted together in their cosmic dance, representing the cycle of creation and rebirth. Other Loa with which he is associated include Ogoun, the warrior Loa, and Legba, the gatekeeper. In Haitian Vodou lore, Damballah is known for his calm and serene demeanor, and his voice is said to be like a gentle breeze, carrying with it the secrets of the universe. He is also known for his great power, strength, and healing abilities and is sometimes called upon in times of illness or distress.

Offerings to Damballah usually consist of pure, clean water and white rum or other white liquors. He is also associated with eggs, as they symbolize fertility and new beginnings. Signs that he has received and accepted offerings include a feeling of peace and calmness and a sense of being in the presence of great wisdom and power. Voodooists celebrate Damballah during the annual Vodou festival, as well as during Mardi Gras and other cultural events. His followers will often dance and chant in his honor, offering prayers and gifts to this powerful and ancient Loa.

Agwe

Agwe, the Loa of the sea, is a powerful and enigmatic figure in the pantheon of Louisiana Voodoo. Known for his fierce loyalty and potent magic, he is revered by sailors, fishermen, and all who make their livelihoods on the waters. Agwe is said to appear as a dark-skinned man with a commanding presence, often dressed in naval or maritime attire. He is associated with the color blue; his symbols include anchors, shells, and fish. His veve is a complex and intricate design featuring waves, seahorses, and a depiction of his sacred vessel, the ship.

In some traditions, Agwe is syncretized with the Catholic saint St. Ulrich of Augsburg, who is said to have miraculous powers over water. However, many practitioners of Louisiana Voodoo view Agwe as a deity in his own right, not to be confused with any other figure. Agwe's correspondences include sea-related items, such as seaweed, coral, sea salt, and the colors blue and white. He is also associated with the herbs vetiver and angelica.

Agwe is connected to his wife, the goddess of love and beauty, Ezili Freda, Baron Samedi, and the Loa of death and rebirth. Agwe's status as a master of the sea often puts him at odds with the Loa of the earth and land, such as Papa Legba and Damballah. Bits of lore connected to Agwe paint him as a powerful and fiercely protective figure, willing to go to great lengths to defend his devotees. He is particularly fond of children, and offerings of toys and candy are often left at his altars as a sign of devotion.

Preferred offerings for Agwe include fish, seafood, and rum, often placed in his sacred vessel, which is kept on his altar. Signs that he has received and accepted an offering may include movement or activity from the sacred vessel and dreams or visions of the sea. Agwe's devotees celebrate him in various ways, including a yearly boat procession down the Mississippi River, known as the Blessing of the Fleet. This event often includes offerings to Agwe and other Loa and traditional music, dancing, and feasting. Devotees may also honor Agwe at home altars or in community gatherings, particularly those associated with the sea or water.

Loko

Loko, the Loa of vegetation, is a powerful spirit who plays an important role in Louisiana Voodoo. He is often depicted as a tall, thin man, wearing a suit made of green leaves and holding a hoe or a machete. Loko's appearance reflects his connection to nature and his role as a farmer who cultivates the land and provides food for the people. Loko's veve, or sacred symbol, is a series of interconnected lines and circles, often depicted in green and brown. This veve is used in ceremonies to invoke Loko's presence and blessings.

In Louisiana Voodoo, Loko is often syncretized with Saint Isidore, the patron saint of farmers. This association highlights the agricultural aspect of Loko's character and his importance in providing for the people. Loko's correspondences include the colors green and brown, as well as plants like corn, beans, and squash, which are traditionally grown together in Native American agriculture. These plants represent Loko's role as a cultivator and provider of sustenance. He has a close relationship with other Loa of agriculture and fertility, such as Ayizan, the Loa of the marketplace, and Azaka, the Loa of the harvest. Together, they ensure the land is fertile, and the people are fed.

You need to beware of this Loa's quick temper and tendency to act impulsively. In some stories, he is portrayed as stubborn and difficult to work with but also fiercely protective of those who honor him. His personality reflects the unpredictability of nature and the challenges faced by those who depend on the land for survival.

To honor Loko, fresh produce offerings, especially corn, are often left at the crossroads or in other outdoor spaces. Signs that Loko has received and accepted an offering may include the rustling of leaves, the sudden appearance of a breeze, or the sound of a hoe striking the ground. Loko is often celebrated in New Orleans during the annual Voodoo Festival and in smaller, more private ceremonies throughout the year. During these ceremonies, participants may sing and dance in honor of Loko, invoking his power to bring abundance and fertility to the land.

Azaka

Azaka, also known as Azaka Medeh, is a Loa associated with agriculture and the earth. He is believed to be a powerful spirit who can bless crops, bring rain, and help the people who rely on the land for their livelihood. He is a tall, muscular man with a muscular physique and the strength of an ox. He is often depicted wearing a straw hat and holding a machete, both symbols of his connection to agriculture. Azaka's veve is a complex symbol that includes the image of a plow and other agricultural tools. It is usually drawn in white on a background of green, which symbolizes fertility and growth.

This powerful Loa is syncretized with Saint Isidore, the patron saint of farmers. This syncretism reflects the importance of agriculture in Haitian society and how traditional beliefs have been incorporated into the practice of Catholicism in Haiti. The colors associated with Azaka are green, brown, and yellow, and his favorite offerings include corn, beans, and other agricultural products. His herbs include basil, vervain, and mugwort, believed to have spiritual and medicinal properties.

Azaka is closely associated with his brother, Guede, who is the Loa of death and the underworld. Together, the two brothers form a powerful duo who are believed to have the ability to bring fertility and abundance to the land. In Haitian Vodou, Azaka is believed to have a jovial and generous personality. He is often seen as a kind and benevolent spirit willing to help those in need. He is especially revered by farmers and those who rely on the land for their livelihood.

To honor Azaka, people often create altars and offer him gifts of food, drink, and tobacco. They may also perform rituals and dances in his honor, particularly during the planting and harvest seasons. In New Orleans, Azaka is celebrated during the annual Vodou Festival, which takes place in the city's historic French Quarter. During the festival, participants pay tribute to the Loa through music, dance, and other forms of artistic expression.

Ogou

Ogou, the powerful warrior Loa of Vodou, is known for his strength, courage, and unyielding character. A fierce protector and defender of the people, he is often invoked for his abilities in battle and as a mediator in disputes. In Vodou tradition, Ogou is often depicted as a handsome, strong, and virile man, dressed in military regalia, with weapons in his hands and a fierce countenance. His image is often associated with red, symbolizing his passion, power, and energy.

The veve of Ogou is a complex symbol, representing his warrior status and association with fire, lightning, and thunder. It is often drawn in a trident shape, symbolizing the three aspects of Ogou; the fiery warrior, the cool-headed mediator, and the deep, wise spirit. Ogou is associated with St. James the Greater in some syncretic traditions, and his feast day is celebrated on July 25th. As a warrior saint, St. James shares many characteristics with Ogou, and many of the stories associated with St. James have been adapted into the mythology of Ogou.

In terms of correspondence, Ogou is often associated with the color red and iron, steel, and other metals. His favorite offerings include rum, cigars, spicy foods, swords, knives, and other weapons. He is also associated with the herb basil, which is said to have protective properties and is often used in offerings and rituals to honor Ogou. Ogou is known to have complex relationships with other Loa. He is often associated with Shango's fiery and passionate spirit and is sometimes seen as a rival to the more seductive and sensual Lwa, Legba. He is also closely connected to the Earth and its elemental forces. He is sometimes associated with the Loa of the crossroads, Papa Legba.

In terms of lore, Ogou is known for his bravery, strength, and keen sense of justice and fairness. He is often called upon to protect the vulnerable and defend the weak and is sometimes associated with the image of the knight in shining armor. When devotees want to honor this Loa, there are many different rituals and practices associated with this powerful and revered Loa. Offerings of rum, tobacco, and spicy foods are often made to Ogou, and he is sometimes invoked in ceremonies involving swords and other weapons. Ogou is often celebrated in New Orleans during Mardi Gras, when many Vodou practitioners honor his powerful and protective spirit with parades, music, and dance.

Ti-Jean Petro

Ti-Jean Petro is a Loa in Louisiana Voodoo who embodies youth, vitality, and the fiery spirit of rebellion. He is often invoked by those seeking to overcome obstacles, stand up for themselves, and make a change in their lives. In appearance, he is often depicted as a young man with dark skin and a muscular build. He may carry a sword, machete, or another weapon and is often seen with a red bandanna or scarf tied around his head. His veve is a complex, interlocking geometric pattern representing his fiery nature and determination. The veve is typically drawn in red or black and is often accompanied by symbols of other Loa with whom Ti-Jean Petro has close connections, such as Papa Legba, Ezili Dantor, and Baron Samedi.

As a Petro Loa, Ti-Jean Petro is not syncretized with any Catholic saints and is instead worshipped in his own right. This Loa's correspondences include red and black and herbs and plants like red pepper, ginger, and tobacco. He is also associated with the elements of fire and water, which symbolize his dual nature as both a fiery spirit of rebellion and a protector of the community. Regarding his relationships with other Loa, Ti-Jean Petro is often seen as a companion to the warrior Loa Ogou. He is also closely connected to Ezili Dantor, the fierce and protective mother figure often invoked by women seeking help with matters of love and protection. Lore connected to Ti-Jean Petro depicts him as a fiery and rebellious spirit who is not afraid to stand up for himself or others. He is known for his fierce determination and willingness to fight for justice and equality.

Offerings of red and black candles, rum, and cigars are often made to honor Ti-Jean Petro. Some practitioners also offer spicy foods, such as hot sauce, to recognize his association with the element of fire. Signs that he has received and accepted your offering may include candles that burn brightly and steadily and a sense of inner strength and determination. Ti-Jean Petro is often celebrated during the annual Voodoo Festival in New Orleans, where he is invoked in ritual and honored with offerings of rum and cigars. In addition, he is often invoked during personal ceremonies and rites, where he is called upon to help individuals overcome obstacles and achieve their goals.

Chapter Seven: Creating Your Voodoo Altar

The Importance of Your Voodoo Altar

You don't have to have a shrine or an altar in your house, but the thing is that having one will increase and strengthen your connection to the spirits. You'll be able to feel them more in your life, and this is a good thing. In the practice of Voodoo, altars are considered the heart and soul of one's spiritual space. They are the place where you can connect the divine, a physical representation of your innermost beliefs, and a visual reminder of the importance of your spiritual practice.

A voodoo altar.[24]

Your altar is your sacred space, and it can be as simple or as elaborate as you want it to be. It can be a small shelf or a large table, and it can hold various items significant to you and your spiritual practice. Altars are a place of worship and reflection where you can seek guidance, solace, or simply a moment of peace.

In Voodoo, altars are not just places to display beautiful objects or decorative pieces. They are a focal point of your practice, where you can offer prayers, make offerings, and invite the spirits to come and dwell with you. You can adorn your altar with candles, flowers, crystals, and other sacred objects that have meaning for you.

It is also important to remember that an altar is a living thing. It is a reflection of your relationship with the spirits, and it must be tended to with care and reverence. You can clean your altar, refresh the offerings, and adjust the placement of items to create a harmonious and peaceful environment. Creating an altar is not just about displaying beautiful objects. A spiritual act of devotion deepens your connection to the divine. It is a space where you can feel free to be yourself, express your hopes and fears, and seek guidance and support. You can light a candle, offer some incense, and sit in quiet contemplation, knowing that you are never alone and the spirits are always with you. So, as you embark on your Voodoo journey, remember the importance of creating a sacred space where you can connect with the spirits. Your altar is a place of reverence, a visual representation of your spiritual practice, and a reminder of the divine presence that surrounds you always.

Choosing a Sacred Space

Creating a Voodoo altar is a sacred act that requires intention and mindfulness. The first step in this process is choosing the perfect space for your altar. You should look for a place that feels peaceful, where you can spend time reflecting and connecting with the spirit world. When selecting a location for your altar, you should consider the energy of the space. Does it feel calm and soothing, or is it chaotic and cluttered? You want to create an altar in a sacred and harmonious space.

Another important consideration is privacy. You want to choose a space where you can set up your altar and perform your rituals without being disturbed. This space should be dedicated solely to your spiritual practice, so you can focus your energy and intentions without any distractions. Remember, the space you choose will be the home of your

Voodoo altar, a place where you will connect with the divine and communicate with the spirits. Choosing a location that feels safe, secure, and welcoming is important. So, take your time, and choose the space that speaks to you. It could be a quiet corner of your bedroom, a cozy nook in your living room, or a peaceful spot in your garden. Wherever you choose, make sure it feels right to you and that it's a space you can dedicate to your spiritual practice for years to come.

Materials Needed

You may wonder why you must create an altar for your Voodoo practice. The answer is simple: it depends on your personal preferences and the Loa with whom you wish to work. However, you can follow some general guidelines to ensure you have what you need.

First of all, it's important to know where to get the materials for your altar. Many items can be found at your local spiritual or metaphysical shop or even online. You can also find items in nature, such as branches, stones, and herbs. But no matter where you get your items, it's important to make sure they are of good quality and resonate with you and your practice. Please note that the items that are required for a Voodoo altar vary, and the items used can depend on the specific tradition or the Loa being honored. However, some common items are typically found on a Voodoo altar.

The centerpiece of a Voodoo altar is usually a large candle, which represents the light of the Loa. The candle should be placed in the center of the altar and should be the tallest item on the altar. The color of the candle can vary depending on the Loa being honored.

The altar itself can be covered with a colored cloth, either red or white, to honor the Petro Loa, or the Rada Loa, respectively.

You can have decorative items like statues, flowers, roots, amulets, talismans, stones, and anything else you resonate with. You'll also want some incense, oils, and even perfumes. Other items that are commonly found on a Voodoo altar include:

- **Water:** Representing the element of water, which is associated with the Loa, water is usually placed in a small dish or bowl on the altar. This water has to be changed every day.
- **Offerings:** Offerings can include food, drink, tobacco, or other items that are pleasing to the Loa. The specific offerings can vary

depending on the Loa being honored.

- **Veve:** You should have the religious symbols representing the Loa you are working with.
- **Gris-gris bags**: Gris-gris bags are small bags filled with herbs, roots, stones, and other objects that are believed to have magical properties. They are often used for protection, luck, or to attract love. You can place the ones that serve your needs on the altar.
- **Ancestral altar:** An ancestral altar is a separate altar dedicated to honoring the spirits of the practitioner's ancestors. It is typically placed near the main Voodoo altar and may include items such as photographs of ancestors, candles, and offerings.

A general rule of thumb is that if something is connected to any of the Loa you're working with or has a deep significance to you and brings you in touch with your spiritual side, you can put it on the altar to enhance its power. Note that you can use a shelf, table, or even a cabinet to set up your altar. You can put up pictures of the Loa, their veves, or the saints with which they are syncretized to draw their energy to your altar. Set a white candle on one side of the altar and a red one on the other side. A bell is another useful item because it immediately raises the vibration of the place when you ring it, and it helps to get rid of any unwanted spirits lurking around.

Blessing and Cleansing Your Items

It is important to cleanse and bless the items you will use to set up your altar. Cleansing removes any negative energy or impurities that may be present while blessing infuses the items with positive energy and the power of the spirits. One cleansing method is to use smoke from burning herbs, such as sage or palo santo. To do this, light the herbs and allow the smoke to permeate the items, saying a prayer or incantation as you do so. For example, you could say, *"Great spirits of the earth and sky, cleanse these items and make them pure. Let them be a sacred offering to you."*

Another method of cleansing is to use salt water. Fill a bowl with water and add a handful of sea salt. Then, dip each item into the salt water and say a prayer or incantation, such as *"May the power of the ocean wash away any negativity from these items and bless them with the power of the sea."* A third method of cleansing is to bury the items in the earth. Find a spot outside, dig a small hole, and bury the items for a few days. This allows the earth to absorb any negative energy and infuse the items with positive energy. When you dig up the items, say a prayer or incantation such as *"Great Mother Earth, bless these items with the power of the Earth and the spirits of the land."*

Once the items have been cleansed, it is important to bless them. One way to do this is to use holy water or a blessing oil. Simply dip your fingers into the water or oil and make the sign of the cross or other symbol on each item. As you do this, say a prayer or incantation, such as *"May these items be blessed by the spirits and be filled with the power of the divine."*

Alternatively, you could use a crystal or other charged object. Hold the crystal in your hand and place the items on top of it, reciting a prayer or incantation, such as "May the power of this crystal bless these items and infuse them with positive energy and the power of the spirits." Suppose you would like a different way to bless the items. In that case, you could use a ritual or ceremony, such as a full moon ceremony or a prayer circle. Gather together with like-minded individuals and say prayers or incantations, asking the spirits to bless the items and fill them with positive energy.

You may be wondering, "What's the big deal if I don't cleanse and bless these things? Why can't I just set up my altar and be done with it?" In Louisiana Voodoo, it is believed that everything has spiritual energy or essence, including the items on your altar. Suppose these items are not properly cleansed and blessed. In that case, they can carry negative or stagnant energy, which can interfere with the effectiveness of your altar and the power of your rituals. Without proper cleansing, any negative energy or intentions which may have been associated with the item, whether during manufacturing or prior usage, could affect your altar negatively. Also, if you do not bless your altar items, you may be missing out on their full potential, as it is believed the *items themselves* have a spiritual essence and can contribute to the effectiveness of your altar and rituals.

Additionally, not properly caring for your altar items can be seen as a lack of respect for the spirits and the practice of Voodoo. This lack of respect and attention to detail can sometimes be seen as disrespectful and may even offend the spirits or ancestors being honored on the altar. So, you have to give proper attention and care to the items on your altar, as they play an integral role in your practice and relationship with the spirits. Properly cleansing and blessing your altar items ensures that they are ready to be used for your rituals and contribute to your practice's overall effectiveness.

Frequently Asked Questions

What is an altar?

An altar is a sacred space to connect with the spirits, ancestors, and the Loa.

Do I need an altar to practice Voodoo?

No, you do not need an altar to practice Voodoo, but it is highly recommended as it provides a focal point for your spiritual practice.

Can I have multiple altars?

Yes, you can have multiple altars for different purposes or to honor different spirits or Loa.

How do I choose a location for my altar?

Choose a location that is quiet and private, where you can focus on your spiritual practice without distraction.

What items should I have on my altar?

The items you should have on your altar depend on the Loa or spirits you are working with, but some common items include candles, water, flowers, statues or pictures of the Loa or spirits, and offerings such as food or drink.

Can I dedicate one altar to two Loa?

Yes, you can dedicate one altar to multiple Loa if they have a strong connection or if they work well together.

Should anyone besides me use my altar?

No, your altar is a personal and sacred space and should only be used by you and those you trust.

Can I decorate my altar with non-traditional items?

Yes, you can decorate your altar with items that have personal significance to you as long as they do not contradict Voodoo's spiritual beliefs and practices.

How do I maintain my altar?

You should regularly clean and tidy your altar, change the water and offerings, and replace any items that have become worn or damaged.

Can I move my altar to a different location?

Yes, you can move your altar to a different location if needed, but you should cleanse and bless the items and space again after the move.

Can I have an outdoor altar?

Yes, you can have an outdoor altar, but you should protect it from the elements and be mindful of any local laws or regulations.

Can I have an altar in a shared space?

Yes, you can have an altar in a shared space, but you should respect the beliefs and practices of those around you and keep the altar clean and tidy.

Can I use a temporary altar?

Yes, you can use a temporary altar if you need to, such as when traveling or if you do not have a permanent space.

Can I have a virtual altar?

Yes, you can have a virtual altar, such as a digital image or a website, but it should still be treated with respect and maintained as you would a physical altar.

How often should I cleanse and bless my altar items?

You should cleanse and bless your altar items regularly, such as once a week or before and after important rituals or offerings.

What is the purpose of cleansing and blessing my altar items?

Cleansing and blessing your altar items remove negative or unwanted energies and imbue them with positive, protective energies to enhance your spiritual practice.

How do I cleanse my altar items?

You can cleanse your altar items using methods such as smoke cleansing with sage or palo santo, saltwater baths, or placing them in direct sunlight or moonlight.

How do I bless my altar items?

You can bless your altar items by speaking prayers or incantations over them, anointing them with oils or holy water, or exposing them to sacred energies or symbols.

Can I use store-bought items on my altar?

Yes, you can use store-bought items. Just make sure you cleanse them first and bless them as well.

Can I keep my altar in a closet or other enclosed space?

It's generally recommended to keep your altar in a space that is open and easily accessible to allow the spirits to interact with it. However, if you need to keep it in a closet or other enclosed space for practical reasons, you can still work with it. Just be careful when working with lit candles.

Can I use herbs and other natural materials for my altar?

Yes, using herbs and other natural materials is a common practice in Voodoo. Just make sure to properly cleanse and bless them before using them on your altar.

Can I use animal bones or other animal parts on my altar?

Using animal bones or other animal parts is a common practice in some forms of Voodoo, but it's important to make sure that the animals are ethically sourced and that you have the proper knowledge and respect for working with them.

Can I use objects from other spiritual practices on my altar?

While some objects from other spiritual practices may be appropriate for your altar, it's important to make sure that they are compatible with Voodoo and that you cleanse and bless them appropriately.

Can I create an altar for a specific purpose or intention, such as healing or prosperity?

Yes, creating an altar for a specific purpose or intention is a common practice in Voodoo. Just make sure to choose items that are appropriate for your intention and to properly cleanse and bless them.

Can I use my altar for divination or other spiritual practices?

Yes, your altar can be used for divination, prayer, and other spiritual practices. Just make sure to properly cleanse and bless the items before using them for each purpose.

Can I use one altar for the Rada and Petro Loa pantheons at the same time?

Please don't do this, as both pantheons are completely different and do not work together like this. You should have different altars, or at the very least, there should be a very clear demarcation on your altar to show one side is for the Petro and the other for the Rada.

Chapter Eight: You and the Wisdom of Your Ancestors

The importance of ancestors in Louisiana Voodoo cannot be overstated. In fact, the practice is founded upon the veneration and worship of those who came before. Ancestors are seen as a bridge between the spiritual and physical realms, a sacred and powerful connection.

In Louisiana Voodoo, the spirits of the ancestors are honored and respected for their guidance, protection, and wisdom. They are believed to watch over their descendants and offer support, love, and blessings to those who honor them. It is believed that your ancestors can impact your life in profound ways, positively or negatively.

Connecting with the elders and the ancestors is crucial to voodoo practice.[25]

Through ancestor worship, the Voodooist seeks to cultivate a relationship with those who have gone before them, tapping into their knowledge and experience to guide them in their own journeys. In turn, devotees offer the ancestors love, respect, and acknowledgment, honoring their presence in their lives and the impact they continue to have on them. The importance of ancestors is evident in the very fabric of Louisiana Voodoo. The use of ancestral altars, rituals, and offerings is a key aspect of the tradition. These altars are adorned with photographs, candles, flowers, and other items that connect you with your ancestors. You can communicate with your ancestors through these offerings, showing them your love and respect and seeking their guidance and wisdom.

The Role of Ancestors

Ancestors play an essential role in the practice, with different types of ancestors being acknowledged and revered. These ancestors include blood, spiritual, and cultural ancestors, and each holds a unique role in the individual's spiritual and physical existence.

Blood ancestors: Blood ancestors are those who are biologically related to the individual, such as grandparents, parents, and siblings. In Louisiana Voodoo, the blood ancestors are believed to watch over and guide their descendants. The individual can access their wisdom and guidance by acknowledging and venerating them.

Spiritual ancestors: These ancestors are those who are not biologically related to the individual but are instead connected through spiritual lineage. They may include Voodoo practitioners, community leaders, or influential spiritual figures. In Louisiana Voodoo, spiritual ancestors are believed to offer their spiritual descendants protection, guidance, and blessings.

Cultural ancestors: Cultural ancestors are those who are connected to the individual through their cultural heritage, such as being African, Native American, or European ancestors. They offer a connection to the individual's roots, heritage, and history and can provide insights into the cultural practices that have shaped their spiritual and physical identity.

Each type of ancestor plays a significant role in the individual's life and spiritual practice, offering a unique perspective and guidance. By acknowledging and venerating each type of ancestor, the individual can develop a deeper connection to their spiritual and cultural heritage and access the wisdom and blessings of those who came before them.

How Your Ancestors Help You

They offer you guidance: Your ancestors can offer guidance in making decisions and navigating life's challenges. They have a wealth of knowledge and experience that they can offer you. They have lived through similar situations and challenges you may be facing and have gained wisdom and insight they can share with you.

By connecting with your ancestors, you are tapping into a source of guidance that can help you make decisions and navigate life's challenges. Your ancestors can guide you in many ways, such as through dreams, intuition, and signs in the physical world. They may also communicate with you through divination tools like tarot cards, pendulums, or spirit boards. These methods can offer you insights, advice, and support to help you make the best decisions for yourself and your life.

They protect you: Your ancestors can offer protection against negative energies and harm. Your ancestors have the power to protect you from negative energies and harm. This protection comes in many forms, including physical, emotional, and spiritual protection. Ancestors can help shield you from danger and negative influences and offer comfort and support when you feel vulnerable or alone.

When you connect with your ancestors, you open up a channel for their protective energy to flow into your life. Inviting them into your practice and dedicating space on your altar for them creates a sacred bond, allowing them to watch over you and keep you safe. Ancestors can also offer protection by helping you recognize and avoid dangerous situations. They benefit from experience and wisdom from their own lives.

They'll help you grow spiritually: Connecting with your ancestors can help you on your spiritual journey and aid in your personal growth. In Louisiana Voodoo, spiritual growth is highly valued and essential to the practice. Ancestors are believed to be highly spiritual beings who have passed on to the spirit world and can guide their descendants on their own spiritual journey. By connecting with their ancestors, Voodoo practitioners can gain valuable insights, wisdom, and understanding of spiritual practices and teachings passed down through generations.

Ancestors, especially those known to be highly spiritual or religious leaders, are believed to have acquired a great deal of spiritual knowledge and experience that can be passed down to their descendants. Through ancestral communication, a practitioner can receive guidance, advice, and teachings that help them develop spiritually and gain a deeper understanding of their spiritual path. Ancestors can also provide reassurance and comfort, helping practitioners find their way during difficult times. Through ancestral communication, you can gain insight into your strengths and weaknesses and identify areas where you need to focus your efforts to continue to grow spiritually. This can lead to deeper self-awareness and help you move forward on your spiritual journey with greater confidence and clarity.

They can help you with manifestation: Your ancestors can assist in manifesting your goals and desires. The ancestors are powerful spiritual beings, able to intervene in the lives of their living descendants. They have a deep connection to the spiritual realm and can act as intermediaries between the physical and spiritual worlds. As a result, they can assist in manifesting the goals and desires of their living descendants. When you connect with your ancestors, you are tapping into the power of your lineage and calling upon your forebears' spiritual strength and abilities. Your ancestors can provide guidance and support to achieve your goals and desires. By working in partnership with them, you can call upon your ancestors to help manifest your intentions.

For example, suppose you're seeking financial abundance. In that case, it's a good idea to connect with those of your ancestors who were known for their business acumen or wealth. You can make offerings and request that your ancestors to guide and bless your financial endeavors. In this way, the ancestors can help to manifest your desires for abundance and success. Your ancestors can be co-creators of your reality along with you if you let them. Working with them is an easier way to live life than going it on your own. You should seek them out not only when you need something; instead, call on them all the time so that the connection between you stays strong.

Rituals for Connecting with Ancestors

Now it's time to connect with your ancestors. Keep in mind that you can switch up your Voodoo altar to make it fit for connecting with your ancestors simply by placing items on it that are reminiscent of them and their interests or that carry their energy. For instance, if you have an item from a late parent or grandparent, you can place it on the altar. The same goes for their photographs. You can also use them as a point of contact for every other ancestor who has passed on before them. With that said, the following are practical rituals that you can use to get in touch with them whenever you need to.

Ancestor Altar Ritual

1. Choose a space for your ancestor altar, such as a corner in your room or a special shelf.
2. Gather materials for your altar, including a white cloth, candles, incense, photos of your ancestors, and any offerings you wish to make.
3. Cleanse and bless your altar items before placing them on the altar, starting with the white cloth on the altar's surface and then placing everything else on it in an orderly fashion. Leave room in the middle of the altar for any item you may want to interact with, so you can set it there and move it aside when done.
4. Light the candles and incense and invite your ancestors to join you by saying a prayer or incantation. Your prayer doesn't have to be anything complex. You could just say, *"My ancestors, you who were here before I drew my first breath, I invite you here and now. Thank you for gracing me with your presence. Thank you for your rapt attention to my desires and for answers to my prayers."*
5. Now, give them any offerings you have chosen. You may do so by simply lifting each one in the air in their honor and placing it on the Center of the altar.
6. If you have anything you'd like to share with them or ask them, now's the time to do so. When you've finished, trust that they've heard you, and you'll get an answer. Also, be sure to thank them.

Ancestor Graveyard Ritual

1. Choose a grave of an ancestor or a local cemetery.
2. Bring offerings such as flowers, candles, food, and drink to leave at the grave.
3. Light candles and incense to create a sacred atmosphere.
4. Speak to your ancestor and offer your gifts and intentions.
5. Listen for any messages or guidance from your ancestor.
6. Thank your ancestor before leaving the cemetery.

Suppose you find cemeteries creepy, but you have an item that once belonged to an ancestor, or you have a picture of them. In that case, you can perform steps 2 to 6 with the image or item. That will also be good enough.

Ancestor Meditation Ritual

1. Find a quiet and comfortable place to sit in front of your ancestor's altar.
2. Light some incense or a candle to create a sacred atmosphere.
3. Close your eyes and take a few deep breaths to center yourself.
4. Visualize a bright light surrounding you, and then imagine your ancestors standing around you, encircling you in their energy.
5. Take a moment to feel their presence and connect with them.
6. Ask your ancestors to share any guidance, wisdom, or messages they have for you.
7. Listen for their response through intuition, visions, or even audible messages. Note that you may not get a response right away. Alternatively, you can just sit and bask in the feeling of appreciation and anticipation that the answer will come to you eventually, either during your meditation or at some point later.
8. When you feel ready, thank your ancestors for their presence and guidance, and offer them water, flowers, or food.
9. Slowly open your eyes and return to the present moment.

Please remember that when it comes to ancestor meditation, "your mileage may vary." Everyone has different experiences, and the odds are you'll need to practice this more than once to connect with your ancestors. So don't be hard on yourself if you feel nothing happened after one try. Consistency, patience, and trust are vital.

Tips for Remaining in Touch

1. Keep a picture of your ancestor on your altar or in a special place in your home where you can see it often. You could have it at the door, so you have to say hello before you leave the house each day.
2. Light a candle or burn some incense in honor of your ancestor every day or on special occasions.

3. Create a special offering for your ancestor, such as a favorite food or drink, and place it on your altar or at their grave site. You could do this weekly. If it's food or drink, you should leave it on the altar for some time, either overnight or just for some hours. Then you can get rid of it by throwing it outside to release the offering to your ancestors.
4. Set aside time each day to meditate and connect with your ancestors. Make this non-negotiable, kind of like brushing your teeth.
5. Write a letter to your ancestor and express your thoughts and feelings. You can either burn it or keep it as a keepsake in a special box dedicated to them. Assume that they will handle whatever you write about that goes into that box.
6. Ask your ancestor for guidance or advice when faced with difficult decisions.
7. Keep a journal to document any signs or messages from your ancestor.
8. Visit your ancestor's grave and bring flowers or other offerings.
9. Create an ancestral altar where you can honor your ancestors and keep their memory alive.
10. Share stories and traditions about your ancestors with your family and friends to keep their memory alive for future generations.

Ethics and Responsibilities of Working with Ancestors

In Louisiana Voodoo, working with ancestors is considered a sacred practice that carries ethical and moral responsibilities. It is believed that when you ask for the help of your ancestors, they respond in kind and offer guidance and protection. However, it is important to remember that with this privilege comes a responsibility to honor and respect your ancestors and their traditions.

One of the most important ethical considerations when working with ancestors is to be clear about your intentions and always ask for their consent before engaging in any rituals or practices. You should never force or coerce your ancestors into doing anything that goes against their will or beliefs. Another key responsibility is to maintain a high level of respect and reverence for your ancestors. This can be done through consistent offerings, such as lighting candles or incense on your altar and regularly performing rituals and prayers in their honor. It is also important to remember that your ancestors may have their own personalities and preferences, and it is important to honor and respect those differences. For example, some ancestors may prefer certain offerings or may not respond well to certain rituals or practices.

Finally, it is crucial to remember that working with ancestors is a two-way street. Just as you seek their guidance and protection, offering them your gratitude and appreciation is important. This can be done through regular offerings and acts of service, such as volunteering or making a charitable donation in their honor.

Now that you understand the importance of involving your ancestors in your daily life as a Voodooist, it's time to look at some of the important items in Voodoo that have been greatly misunderstood – so you know exactly how to make them work for you.

The next chapter will shed light on charms and more.

Chapter Nine: Voodoo Dolls and Charms

So, if you've learned anything about Voodoo, you probably already know about the Voodoo doll, the most popular of the charms. However, other charms are part of New Orleans Voodoo, and you're going to learn about them and more in this chapter.

Voodoo dolls.[26]

The Voodoo Doll

You must have heard of the Voodoo doll before, the tiny rag doll used to cast spells or cause harm to someone. But the reality of Voodoo dolls is quite different from the stereotype portrayed in movies and TV shows. A Voodoo doll is a handmade doll representing a person, typically used for healing, blessing, or protection. The doll is imbued with the energy of the person it represents and is believed to be a physical manifestation of that person. It is not used to cause harm or cast spells but to help connect with the person the doll represents.

Historically, in West Africa, dolls were used in religious ceremonies to represent ancestors or deities. When enslaved Africans were brought to the Americas, they brought their spiritual traditions with them, including the use of dolls in religious practices. Over time, the use of dolls evolved and adapted to the new environment and eventually became an integral part of Louisiana Voodoo. Unfortunately, the portrayal of Voodoo dolls in popular culture has created a number of misconceptions. Many people believe that Voodoo dolls are used to cause harm or control others, but this is simply not true. Louisiana Voodoo is a religion that emphasizes healing, protection, and connection with ancestors and spirits, not harm or manipulation. So, the next time you see a Voodoo doll in a movie or on TV, remember that it's not an accurate representation of the beautiful and complex spiritual practices of Louisiana Voodoo.

Gris-Gris

A *gris-gris* is a very powerful charm used in Louisiana Voodoo. It's a small bag filled with various objects, such as herbs, stones, and other curios, that are believed to hold spiritual power. This charm is used for various purposes, including protection, luck, love, and even to cause harm to an enemy. Gris-gris is rooted in African spiritual traditions that were brought to the Americas during the slave trade. The practice of using charms or amulets to protect oneself from evil spirits or bad luck has been around for centuries, and gris-gris is just one of many examples.

One common misconception about gris-gris is that it's always used for evil purposes. While it's true that gris-gris can be used to cause harm to an enemy, it's often used for more positive purposes, such as protection and luck. Another misconception is that gris-gris bags are always made by a Voodoo priest or priestess. While it's true that some gris-gris bags are made by practitioners with special training, it's also possible to make your own gris-gris at home.

So, don't be afraid of gris-gris. It's a fascinating and powerful charm that can be used for a variety of purposes. Just make sure that you're using it for the right reasons and with the proper guidance.

Mojo Bags

First, a mojo bag is not a cute little accessory to add to your outfit; it is a powerful tool used in Louisiana Voodoo and hoodoo traditions. A mojo bag is essentially a small, magical bag that contains certain ingredients, such as herbs, roots, crystals, or personal items, which are believed to bring luck, protection, love, or any other desired outcome. These bags are also known as "mojo hands" or "conjure bags," depending on the specific tradition.

In the past, slaves and other marginalized groups used mojo bags for protection and empowerment. They would create these bags using whatever materials they had on hand, including herbs, roots, and personal items such as hair or clothing. They believed carrying these bags would help them overcome obstacles and bring good luck. However, despite its historical significance, there are still some common misconceptions about mojo bags; just like gris-gris, some assume mojo bags are bad news. The truth is you can use them for either good or bad. It all comes down to your intentions, which are hopefully good.

Materials and Tools for Crafting Charms

When it comes to making charms, whether that's a Voodoo doll, gris-gris, or mojo bag, there are a variety of materials that you can use to create something very powerful and effective. Some common materials include:

- **Herbs:** Different herbs can represent different things, such as rosemary for protection or lavender for healing.
- **Oils:** Essential oils can anoint the charm and imbue it with certain energies or properties.
- **Stones:** Crystals and other stones can enhance the doll's energy and add specific qualities, such as amethyst for spiritual protection or citrine for abundance.
- **Cloth:** The color of the cloth you choose can also have significance. For example, red cloth may be used for love or

passion, while green for prosperity.

- **Charms:** Small trinkets can be added to the Voodoo doll, gris-gris, or mojo bag to enhance its power. For example, a small key could be added to attract success or money. You can also add other charms together to give it more oomph.
- **Other materials:** Other materials that you may want to consider include feathers, shells, or other items that hold personal significance to you.

In addition to materials, you will also need some tools to create your Voodoo doll. Some common tools include:

- **Needle and thread:** You'll need these to sew the doll, mojo bag, or gris-gris together.
- **Scissors:** These will be necessary to cut the fabric and any other materials you'll be using.
- **Pins:** Pins can help hold things in place as you sew.
- **Stuffing:** You'll need something to stuff your doll with. Some people use cotton or other soft materials, while others prefer herbs or other materials to give the doll additional supernatural properties.
- **Mortar and pestle:** Used to grind herbs into a fine powder.
- **Anointing tool:** This could be a small brush. You could also just use a finger to anoint the charm with oil.

Choosing the appropriate materials is key to creating an effective charm. You'll want to consider your intentions and choose materials that align with your goals. For example, suppose you're making a charm for protection. In that case, you may want to choose materials like angelica root and chili peppers, which are known for their protective properties. If you're making a charm for love, you may want to choose materials like rose petals or rose oil – which are associated with love and romance. Remember, the more intentional you are with your materials, the more powerful your charm will be.

How to Make a Voodoo Doll

Materials:
- A piece of fabric in the color of your choice
- A needle and thread
- Stuffing material (cotton, wool, or similar)
- Herbs, stones, oils, or other items to use as embellishments or to match your intentions
- Scissors
- Cleansing and blessing tools (such as sage or palo santo)

Steps:
1. Begin by cleansing your workspace and tools with sage or palo santo. This will help to clear any negative energy and prepare the space for your intention.
2. Choose the fabric you want to use for your doll. The color and type of fabric can vary depending on your intentions. Red is often used for love and passion, green for money and abundance, and white for purification and healing. Cut out two identical pieces of fabric into the shape of your doll.
3. Place the two pieces of fabric on top of each other with the wrong sides facing outward. Sew them together around the edges, leaving a small opening for stuffing.
4. Turn the fabric right-side-out. This will hide the stitching and give you a clean surface to work with.
5. Stuff the doll with the stuffing material. Be sure to pack it tightly, but not so tightly that the doll loses shape.
6. Stitch up the opening you left for stuffing.
7. Now, it's time to add the embellishments. This can be anything from herbs, stones, or oils to match your intention. Use a needle and thread to attach these items to the doll, being mindful of the placement and symbolism of each item.
8. Once you have finished adding the embellishments, hold the doll in your hands and say a prayer or blessing over it. Ask your ancestors or deities to imbue the doll with the energy of your intention.

9. Breathe over your doll thrice. This is meant to activate the doll's energy and set it to work on your intentions and prayers.
10. Your Voodoo doll is now complete and can be used in your spiritual practice.

Remember to keep your intention clear and focused while creating the doll, and use materials that match that intention. This will help to ensure that a doll is a powerful tool in your spiritual practice. You can refer to the chapter on the various oils, herbs, and roots you can use for your doll.

Making a Gris-Gris

Materials:
- Small cloth or leather pouch
- Herbs, roots, and/or stones appropriate for your intentions
- Personal items, such as hair or fingernail clippings
- Ribbon or string for tying the pouch closed
- Needle and thread
- Scissors

Steps:
1. Choose a small cloth or leather pouch for your gris-gris. It should be large enough to hold your chosen ingredients but small enough to be easily carried with you.
2. Based on your intentions, decide on the specific herbs, roots, and/or stones you want to use for your gris-gris. You may want to research the correspondences of different herbs and stones to make the most appropriate choice.
3. Cleanse and bless your materials before beginning. You may want to say a prayer or recite a chant for this purpose.
4. Lay out all your materials in front of you, so they are easily accessible.
5. Take the pouch and begin to fill it with your chosen ingredients. Add the herbs, roots, and/or stones and any personal items you want to include. As you add each item, focus on your intentions and visualize them coming to fruition.
6. Once you have added all of your materials, tie the pouch closed with ribbon or string. You may want to knot it several times to

ensure that it stays closed.
7. Use a needle and thread to sew the pouch closed, sealing your intentions inside. As you do this, focus your energy on your desires and visualize them coming to fruition.
8. When you have finished sewing the pouch closed, cleanse and bless the gris-gris once again. You may want to recite a prayer or chant for this purpose.
9. Breathe thrice on the gris-gris satchel to activate its power.
10. Keep the gris-gris with you at all times, or place it in a location where you will see it regularly. You may want to recharge it periodically by holding it and focusing your energy on your intentions.

Please remember that these are just basic instructions. You may want to modify them based on your preferences and practices. It's also important to remember that gris-gris and other charms should be used ethically and responsibly with the intention of benefiting yourself and others.

Making a Mojo Bag

Materials:
- Cloth
- Needle and thread
- Your preferred herbs
- Your preferred oils
- Talismans (may include gris-gris)
- Personal effects
- A drawstring or regular string
- Petition paper (paper with your intention written on it)

Steps:
1. First, take the cloth and cut out a rectangular piece. Fold that cut-out cloth in half.
2. Next, stitch the folded cloth on only three sides so that you have one side open. That open side is where your drawstring will go.
3. Turn the sewn bag inside out. Around the open side of the bag, create a seam.

4. Stitch the open seam, remembering to cut out two little holes to allow the drawstring to pass through it. Slide the drawstring in, holding on to it through the bag as you push it till it comes out the other hole.
5. Pick the oils, talismans, herbs, and other things you want to put into the bag. Make sure you're choosing items that match the intention you have.
6. Place your petition paper with your intention into the bag.
7. Breathe thrice over everything in the bag. This is meant to activate the bag's power and set it to work on your intention right away.
8. Pull on the drawstring till the bag is secured shut. Then knot the drawstring thrice.
9. Take the bag to your altar and pray to the Loa and your ancestors that they make your desire come to pass. You may anoint it with oil if you wish.
10. When you're done, place it somewhere out of sight of other people. You may sleep with it under your pillow each night if you wish.

Note that you can use these charms for anything you desire, whether it's finances, health, emotional well-being, protection, provision, increase in spiritual power, getting rid of bad luck, increasing good luck, and so on.

Disposing of Your Charm

When your charm has achieved the intention you set for it, you may want to dispose of it. Here's how:

- First, offer thanks to the charm for all it's done for you. Also, thank your ancestors and the Loa.
- Tell the charm that it's time for it to release the power that it has and stop working. Then light a candle or some incense and burn it by the charm to express your gratitude and release its power.
- When you've finished, remove all the personal effects you've got in the charm, whether it's fingernails, hair, pictures, and so on. You may keep them if you wish or dispose of them somewhere away from the charm.
- Finally, it's time to dispose of the charm. For negative charms or charms meant to get rid of bad situations, you should either burn

them or throw them into a running stream or river. If it was a charm meant to bring good things or for good intentions, you can bury it somewhere near a tree to give off its good energy there, or you may burn it if you wish.

Let's Talk Ethics

Ethics are basically the morals that everyone lives by. They're what people use to determine the right choices to make. The codes of ethics differ from one religious practice to another. Still, generally, the common themes include responsibility, respect, justice, honesty, compassion, and fairness. Here are some general guidelines when it comes to the ethics of working with charms.

1. **Please use these charms only for good intentions.** You have to pause and ask yourself if your reasons are justified before you make and use the charms. It's okay to use them for success, peace, protection, love, and things of that nature, but it's not okay to use them to curse or hurt someone, especially if you have no valid reason to do so.

2. **Please do your best to honor the deep meaning of every ingredient you choose to put into the charm.** Once more, revisit the chapter that lets you know the significance of herbs, roots, and colors. You can also do some further research so you can learn more about what's okay to use and how to ethically acquire the materials.

3. **You should always breathe onto your charm.** This will give it life and have it begin working for you. This activation is absolutely vital.

4. **If you come across someone else's charm somehow, please don't touch it or attempt to use it.** If you're curious, seek permission first before asking questions or touching the items.

5. **You should always pray to your Loa and ancestors to let them know what your intentions are for the charms.** Tell them what results you want to get. Trust that they will help you. Keep in mind that you're to interact with them respectfully, so don't try to command them to do things for you. Stay humble, and keep an appreciative vibe about yourself.

6. **You can and should consider recharging your charms.** You can do this by saying prayers over them or by anointing them with oil. You can do this regularly. It's also a good idea to speak to your charm as

if it were an actual person because it does have its own consciousness. If the thought of speaking to your charm feels odd to you, you should pause and remind yourself of the fact that all things are created by Bondye, and all things are filled with his light and life. There's nothing weird about talking to your charm. After all, Bondye created you and spoke to you through his Loa — and he doesn't think it's weird.

Working with charms is a powerful way to practice Voodoo and make it a very real thing in your daily life.

So, take a moment to think about your greatest desires. What might you be able to make a charm for? Go for it!

Chapter Ten: Voodoo Spells and Rituals to Try

In the rhythms of Voodoo, there is a sacred structure to the rituals that have been passed down from generations before. As in a dance, the steps are not only felt but known in the heart, and it is with reverence that each movement is made. The four distinct phases of a ritual are:

- Preparation
- Invocation
- Possession
- Farewell

First, the preparation begins. It is a time of cleansing, both of the body and of the spirit. Bathing with herbs and oils to purify the self, sweeping the space to rid it of negative energy, and lighting candles and incense to call in the spirits. This is the time to set intentions and connect with the divine.

Next, the invocation begins. Here is where the spirits are called forth. Each Loa, or spirit, has its own veve, a symbol that is drawn on the ground with cornmeal or flour, and offerings are made to honor them. The veve acts as a gateway for the Loa to enter the physical realm, and through this gateway, they may communicate with the Voodooist. The Loa are not the only ones summoned from the spirit realm. Voodooists also call out to their ancestors to participate in the events unfolding.

Then comes the time of possession. The Loa enters the body of the chosen person, often called the "horse," and through this vessel, they can communicate with the human realm. The horse may dance or speak in tongues, and through this ecstatic experience, the connection with the divine is strengthened.

Finally, comes the farewell. This is the time to release the spirits back to their realm to give thanks for their presence and guidance. The offerings made during the invocation are given to the spirits, and the veve is erased, closing the gateway between the two worlds. In this way, the Voodoo ritual is like a prayer, a song that is sung to connect with the divine. It is a sacred dance, a communication with the spirits that have been present since the beginning of time.

Now you understand the basic structure of spells and rituals in Voodoo, it's time for you to practice some spells and get the hang of things. Let's start with some powerful protection spells. Please don't freak out at the "possession" steps because it's just about letting the energy of your intention, the Loa, ancestors, and all the materials you're working with to flow through you. If you can't feel it, just imagine you can, and visualize it as a beautiful light coursing through your body.

Protection Spells

Shield Protection Spell

Materials:

- 1 white candle
- 1 black candle
- 1 small bag of sea salt
- 1 amulet of St. Michael
- 1 piece of cypress wood
- 1 piece of black cloth
- 1 piece of white cloth

Preparation:

1. Find a quiet and safe space to perform the ritual.
2. Cleanse the space with burning sage or palo santo.

Invocation:
1. Light the white candle to represent the purity and protection of your ancestors and loved ones.
2. Light the black candle to represent the negative energies you wish to banish and protect yourself from.
3. Sprinkle sea salt around the space to purify and protect it.
4. Call upon the powerful and protective spirit of St. Michael to assist you in this ritual. You can say, *"St. Michael, I call upon you to protect and shield me from all harm. Please lend me your strength and courage to face any obstacles that come my way."*
5. Invoke the spirit of Baron Samedi, the Loa of death and protector of the cemetery, by placing the piece of cypress wood on the altar. You can say, *"Baron Samedi, I call upon your power to protect me from any spiritual harm that may come my way. I ask that you bless this piece of cypress wood and imbue it with your protective energies."*

Possession:
1. Take the piece of cypress wood and wrap it in the white cloth.
2. Place the amulet of St. Michael on top of the cypress wood.
3. Wrap the cypress wood and amulet in the black cloth.
4. Hold the bundle in your hands and envision a white light surrounding you, protecting you from all negative energies. Feel this energy taking over your body and mind, "possessing" you, flooding you with its power.
5. Tie the bundle with a black string or thread and place it in a safe and sacred place.

Farewell:
1. Thank Baron Samedi and St. Michael for their assistance and protection.
2. Extinguish the candles and dispose of them safely.
3. Thank your ancestors for their protection and guidance.
4. Sprinkle sea salt around the perimeter of the space to close and seal the ritual.

Bayou Protection Bath

Materials:
- Florida water
- Rosemary (or any protective herb)
- Dried rose petals
- 1 tablespoon black salt
- 1 white candle
- Rosemary oil (or any protective oil)

Preparation:
1. Start by cleansing your bathroom with Florida water or any protective herb like sage or rosemary.
2. Draw a hot bath and add a handful of dried rose petals, a tablespoon of black salt, and a pinch of protective herbs like bay leaves, basil, or mint.
3. Light a white candle on the side of the tub and place a small bowl of water on the other side.

Invocation:
1. Call upon Papa Legba, the Loa who acts as the gatekeeper between the worlds, to open the doors and offer his protection. You can recite a chant or prayer such as, *"Papa Legba, guardian of the crossroads, I call upon you to open the way and keep me safe from harm. Let your light guide me through the shadows and keep me protected in your hands."*
2. Invoke your ancestors by calling out their names and asking them to offer their guidance and protection during this ritual.

Possession:
1. Get into the tub and let the warm water embrace you. Close your eyes and focus on your intention to be protected from harm, negativity, and anything that might threaten your well-being.
2. Pour a few drops of protective oil, such as rosemary, lavender, or frankincense, on your forehead, chest, and feet.
3. Visualize a shield of white light surrounding you, repelling any negativity and creating a barrier of protection.

Farewell:

1. When you feel ready, thank Papa Legba and your ancestors for their protection and guidance.
2. Drain the bathwater, and sprinkle a handful of black salt around the drain to seal the protection.
3. Blow out the candle and discard the leftover herbs outside of your house.

Note: This bath can be done anytime you feel the need for protection, but it is particularly useful during the waning moon or in times of stress, anxiety, or uncertainty. Use a white candle for purity, clarity, and protection. You can also use other colors that correspond to your intention, such as black for banishing negativity, purple for spiritual protection, or green for physical protection. Use oils that have protective properties, such as rosemary for purification, lavender for peace, or frankincense for spiritual strength. Bay leaves are known for their protective powers, and they also add a pleasant scent to the bath.

For Health

Healing Waters of Loco

Materials:

- 1 white candle
- 1 cup of fresh water
- 1 white cloth
- 1 small pouch with tobacco, mint, and comfrey (you may just use one of these herbs)
- Peppermint oil (you may use eucalyptus or lavender instead)

Preparation:

1. Gather the necessary supplies.
2. Cleanse yourself and your space with a smudge of sage or palo santo.
3. Dress the candle with oil.

Invocation:

1. Light the white candle and place it on a white cloth.

2. Call upon Loco, the Loa of healing and transformation, by reciting his prayer and invoking his veve with white chalk or flour on the ground:

"Great Loco, spirit of the winds and the trees, I humbly ask for your healing touch. May your gentle winds bring me the soothing balm of your grace, and may your mighty strength transform me from illness to wholeness. Loco, I call upon you to join me in this sacred space, to bless and protect me, and to guide me on the path of healing."

3. Sprinkle Loco's herbs and roots around the candle and the white cloth.

Possession:

1. Pour the cup of fresh water into the pouch of herbs and roots and let it steep for a few minutes.
2. Close your eyes and visualize Loco's energy flowing through your body, cleansing and healing you from any physical or emotional ailment.
3. Open the pouch and pour the healing water over your head and body, letting it wash away any negative energy or sickness. You can recite Loco's name or prayer while bathing in the healing water.
4. When you feel fully immersed in the healing energy of Loco, extinguish the candle.

Farewell:

1. Thank Loco for his blessings and healing power, and bid him farewell with gratitude and respect.
2. Dispose of the herbs and roots in a natural setting, such as a garden or a forest.

Keep the white cloth as a reminder of the healing ritual, and carry the pouch of herbs and roots with you for continued protection and healing.

Loco's Healing Candle Spell

Materials:

- 1 white candle
- Pen and paper
- A drop of bayberry oil
- A pinch of ginger root

- A pinch of hyssop
- A pinch of rosemary

Preparation:
1. Begin by preparing your space. Clear the area of any clutter or distractions, and make sure that you have all the materials you need.
2. Light the white candle and take a few deep breaths to center yourself.

Invocation:
1. Next, call upon Loco by reciting the following invocation:
2. *"Great Loco, spirit of healing, hear my call. I ask that you bless me with your healing energy and restore my body, mind, and soul to full health. I call upon you, Loco, to aid me in this time of need."*

Possession:
1. Take the piece of paper and write down any health issues or concerns you are currently facing. Place the paper in front of the candle.
2. Take a drop of bayberry oil and anoint the candle, starting at the top and working your way down to the base. As you anoint the candle, focus on the intention of healing and imagine Loco's healing energy filling the space.
3. Take a pinch of ginger root, hyssop, and rosemary and sprinkle them around the candle.
4. Light the candle and focus your attention on the flame. Visualize the healing energy of Loco coming through the flame and into your body, filling you with vitality and strength.
5. Repeat the following chant three times:

   "Loco, great healer, I call upon your power.

   Bring forth your energy, in this healing hour.

   Restore my health, and make me strong.

   Great Loco, heal me, and right what is wrong."

Farewell:
1. Once the candle has completely burned down, dispose of the remains and thank Loco for his healing energy.
2. Close the ritual with the following statement:

"As I blow out this candle, my ritual is done.
But Loco's healing energy will continue on.
Thank you, Loco, for your presence and aid.
I am now healed, in your power and name."

This ritual utilizes the white candle, which represents purity and clarity, and the herbs of ginger root, hyssop, and rosemary, which are known for their healing properties. Bayberry oil is also used to anoint the candle, which is known for its protective and healing qualities.

For Finances
Abundant Blessings Spell

Materials:
- 1 green candle
- Chamomile and bay leaves
- Ginger root
- Basil oil
- A small green bag or sachet
- A small piece of paper and a pen

Preparation:
1. Cleanse the space where the ritual will take place.
2. Set up an altar with the green candle in the center, and the chamomile and bay leaves, ginger root, basil oil, and a small bag or sachet on the altar.
3. Light the green candle.

Invocation:
1. Call upon Papa Legba, the Loa who opens the doors to opportunity, with the following chant:

    "Papa Legba, guardian of the crossroads,
    Hear my call and open the way.
    Bless me with abundance and prosperity,
    And guide me to success each day."

2. Take a few moments to meditate on your intention of calling forth abundance and prosperity and visualizing the flow of wealth and

resources in your life.

Possession:
1. On the small piece of paper, write down your intention and desires for prosperity and abundance.
2. Anoint the paper with basil oil, and place it in the small green bag or sachet.
3. Add the chamomile and bay leaves, and ginger root to the bag or sachet.
4. Hold the bag or sachet in your hands, and focus your energy and intention of calling forth abundance and prosperity.
5. Chant the following:
    "Abundance and prosperity flow to me,
    Wealth and success come easily.
    As I will, so it be."

Farewell:
1. Thank Papa Legba for his assistance and guidance.
2. Extinguish the green candle.

Keep the green bag or sachet on your person or in a safe, sacred space to continue manifesting abundance and prosperity in your life.

Ezili's Abundance Bath

Materials:
- 8 green candles
- Patchouli oil
- Cinnamon powder
- Bay leaves
- Money, preferably in the form of coins

Preparation:
1. Cleanse the bathroom area by sweeping the floor and washing the surfaces with mild soap and water.
2. Set up the green candles around the bathtub, placing them in a circle.
3. Light the candles and turn off any artificial lights.

Invocation:
1. Call upon your ancestors for their guidance and protection during the ritual.
2. Call upon the Loa Ezili Freda, known for her ability to bring wealth and prosperity, to join the ritual and offer her blessings.

Possession:
1. Pour warm water into the bathtub and add a few drops of patchouli oil to the water.
2. Sprinkle cinnamon powder and crushed bay leaves into the water to draw in abundance and prosperity.
3. Visualize yourself surrounded by wealth and abundance. See it in your mind's eye as green energy possessing you, filling you up.
4. Get into the bathtub and soak in the water for at least 20 minutes, focusing on your intentions for financial abundance and prosperity.
5. As you soak, take the coins and toss them into the water, visualizing them multiplying and growing in value.

Farewell:
1. When you have finished, stand up and let the water drain from the tub, visualizing any blockages or negative energies being removed with the water.
2. Extinguish the candles and thank Ezili Freda and your ancestors for their guidance and blessings.

Note: The green candles and bay leaves represent wealth and money, while the patchouli oil is believed to draw in abundance. Cinnamon is used for its energy-boosting properties. By invoking Ezili Freda, you seek the Loa's aid in manifesting wealth and prosperity. Finally, the act of tossing coins into the water is a symbolic gesture of attracting money and prosperity.

For Love

Bain d'Amour (Bath of Love)

Materials:
- 2 pink candles
- A handful of rose petals

- 1 cup of honey
- ½ cup of olive oil
- ½ cup of lavender oil
- ½ cup of cinnamon powder
- 1 red apple
- 1 piece of paper and a pen

Preparation:
1. Cleanse yourself and the bathroom before beginning the ritual.
2. Light the pink candles and place them in a safe location in the bathroom.
3. Cut the red apple into small pieces and set it aside.
4. Write your name and the name of your desired partner on the piece of paper.

Invocation:
1. Sit in front of the candles and take three deep breaths to center yourself.
2. Call upon the Loa Ezili Freda to bless your ritual bath for love.
3. Hold the piece of paper with the names in your hand and speak your intentions for the ritual.
4. Sprinkle rose petals around the candles and on the bathroom floor, creating a path to the bath.
5. Add the cinnamon powder to the bathwater.

Possession:
1. Pour the honey, olive oil, and lavender oil into the bathwater while stirring clockwise.
2. Place the apple pieces in the bathwater.
3. Enter the bath and immerse yourself fully in the water.
4. Visualize yourself in a loving and committed relationship with your desired partner. Speak your intentions out loud or in your mind.
5. Stay in the bath for at least 15 minutes, focusing on your intentions and feeling the energy of the ritual.
6. After you have finished, step out of the bath and let the water drain away.

Farewell:

1. Thank Ezili Freda and your ancestors for their presence and assistance.
2. Snuff out the candles and discard any leftover materials from the bath.
3. Carry the piece of paper with the names on it with you until your intentions manifest.
4. Give the remaining apple pieces as an offering to nature or bury them in the ground.

Note: The candle colors that match the intention of the ritual are pink, which represents love and romance. The herbs and oils that match the intention are rose petals, lavender oil, and cinnamon powder, which all have properties associated with love and attraction. Ezili Freda is the Loa associated with love, beauty, prosperity, and femininity, making her an appropriate choice for this ritual. As with all Voodoo rituals, it is important to call upon one's ancestors for guidance and protection.

For Luck

Lucky Hand Spell

Materials:

- Green candle
- Lucky Hand root
- Five Finger Grass
- Cinnamon oil
- Patchouli oil

Preparation:

1. Set up a clean and quiet space for the ritual.
2. Gather all of the materials needed.
3. Dress the green candle with a mixture of cinnamon and patchouli oils.
4. Place the Lucky Hand root and Five Finger Grass in a bowl or dish.

Invocation:

1. Light the green candle and place it in front of you.

2. Hold the Lucky Hand root in your left hand and the Five Finger Grass in your right hand.
3. Close your eyes and take a deep breath, clearing your mind.
4. Call upon the Loa Ezili Danto, who is associated with good luck and prosperity, by saying:

   "Ezili Danto, powerful Loa of good luck, I call upon you to bless me with your divine presence. Hear my prayer, grant me your protection, and bestow upon me the power of good fortune."
5. Hold the Lucky Hand root and Five Finger Grass up to the candle flame, allowing the heat to release their scents and energies.
6. Take the Lucky Hand root and anoint it with the cinnamon oil, saying: *"As I anoint this Lucky Hand root, I invite the spirits of good luck and prosperity to guide me."*
7. Take the Five Finger Grass and anoint it with the patchouli oil, saying: *"As I anoint this Five Finger Grass, I invite the spirits of opportunity and success to guide me."*

Possession:

1. Place the Lucky Hand root and Five Finger Grass in a small pouch or bag, and feel their energy as you hold the bag in your hands. You can carry it with you for good luck.

Farewell:

1. Blow out the candle and thank Ezili Danto for her presence and blessings.
2. Close the ritual by saying: *"Thank you, Ezili Danto, for your divine presence and blessings. I ask for your continued guidance and protection. I honor the spirits of good luck and prosperity and give thanks for their assistance. My ritual is now complete."*

These are just a handful of spells you can try out right away. Don't have a certain material? You can always replace it with something else that serves the same purpose. With these spells, you should have an idea of how to create your own rituals for any other purposes you might have that aren't mentioned in this book. It's also helpful to research and learn more about spellwork in Louisiana Voodoo, so your confidence can grow as you practice, and you can have phenomenal results. Do your spells with great respect for the spirits, and be sincere about whatever you need them to help you with.

Conclusion

We've finally come to the end of this book. Now, you know everything you need to begin your journey as a Voodooist. As you have come to the end of this journey exploring the world of New Orleans Voodoo in these pages (and the start of a new one exploring it in your life), you might feel a deep sense of awe and reverence for this profound spiritual practice. Through this book, you have delved into the history, rituals, spells, and religious tenets of Louisiana Voodoo and have been left with a profound understanding of the beauty and power of this practice.

One of the most important takeaways from this book is the importance of sincerity in one's spiritual practice. New Orleans Voodoo is not simply a collection of spells and rituals to be performed without intention or understanding. It is a living, breathing spiritual tradition that requires deep reverence and respect for the spirits, ancestors, and deities that are central to its practice.

You have seen how New Orleans Voodoo emerged from the rich cultural tapestry of Louisiana, combining elements of African spirituality, Catholicism, and Native American traditions. New Orleans Voodoo is a practice shaped by the struggles and triumphs of its people and has given rise to a unique and powerful spiritual tradition.

At the heart of New Orleans Voodoo is the belief in the interconnection of all things. The spirits, ancestors, and deities central to its practice are seen as living entities that can communicate with and guide those seeking their aid. Through rituals, spells, and offerings, practitioners seek to forge a deep spiritual connection with these beings and tap into their wisdom, guidance, and power.

This sense of connection and community makes New Orleans Voodoo a profound and transformative practice. Through your exploration of this tradition, you have seen how it has given solace, guidance, and healing to those who seek its aid. It is a practice that honors the rich diversity of our human experience and offers a path to spiritual growth and transformation.

Approach the practice of New Orleans Voodoo with sincerity, reverence, and respect. Trust in the power of the spirits, and allow yourself to be guided by their wisdom and guidance. Remember that this spiritual tradition requires dedication and commitment, but the rewards are immeasurable.

May the spirits guide and protect you on your journey, and may the practice of New Orleans Voodoo bring you the healing, prosperity, love, and good luck you seek. Walk with grace, power, and love, knowing that all are connected, and the spirits are always with you.

Here's another book by Mari Silva that you might like

Your Free Gift
(only available for a limited time)

Thanks for getting this book! If you want to learn more about various spirituality topics, then join Mari Silva's community and get a free guided meditation MP3 for awakening your third eye. This guided meditation mp3 is designed to open and strengthen ones third eye so you can experience a higher state of consciousness. Simply visit the link below the image to get started.

https://spiritualityspot.com/meditation

Or, Scan the QR code!

References

Desmangles, L. (1992). The Faces of the Gods: Vodou and Roman Catholicism in Haiti. University of North Carolina Press.

Fandrich, I. J. (2005). The Birth of New Orleans' Voodoo Queen: A Long-Held Mystery Resolved. Louisiana History

Fandrich, I. J. (2007). Yorùbá influences Haitian vodou and New Orleans voodoo. Journal of Black Studies.

Filan, K. (2010). The Haitian Vodou Handbook: Protocols for Riding with the Lwa. Destiny Books.

Guenin-Lelle, D. (2016). The Story of French New Orleans: History of a Creole City. Univ. Press of Mississippi.

Hazzard-Donald, K. (2012). Mojo workin': The old African American hoodoo system. University of Illinois Press.

Hebblethwaite, B. (2012). Vodou Songs in Haitian Creole and English. Temple University Press.

Hurston, Z. (1931). Hoodoo in America. The Journal of American Folklore.

McAlister, E. (2002). Rara! Vodou, Power, and Performance in Haiti and its Diaspora. University of California Press.

Murphy, J. (2011). Working the Spirit: Ceremonies of the African Diaspora. Beacon Press.

Packham, J. (2012). Voodoo. The Encyclopedia of the Gothic.

Stewart, L. (2017). Work the Root: Black Feminism, Hoodoo Love Rituals, and Practices of Freedom. Hypatia.

Touchstone, B. (1972). Voodoo in new Orleans. Louisiana History: The Journal of the Louisiana Historical Association

Brown, K. (2001). Mama Lola: A Vodou Priestess in Brooklyn. University of California Press.

Desmangles, L. (1992). The Faces of the Gods: Vodou and Roman Catholicism in Haiti. University of North Carolina Press.

Fandrich, I. J. (2005). The Birth of New Orleans' Voodoo Queen: A Long-Held Mystery Resolved. Louisiana History

Fandrich, I. J. (2007). Yorùbá influences on Haitian vodou and New Orleans voodoo. Journal of Black Studies.

Filan, K. (2010). The Haitian Vodou Handbook: Protocols for Riding with the Lwa. Destiny Books.

Guenin-Lelle, D. (2016). The Story of French New Orleans: History of a Creole City. Univ. Press of Mississippi.

Hebblethwaite, B. (2012). Vodou Songs in Haitian Creole and English. Temple University Press.

McAlister, E. (2002). Rara! Vodou, Power, and Performance in Haiti and its Diaspora. University of California Press.

Murphy, J. (2011). Working the Spirit: Ceremonies of the African Diaspora. Beacon Press.

Packham, J. (2012). Voodoo. The Encyclopedia of the Gothic.

Touchstone, B. (1972). Voodoo in new Orleans. Louisiana History: The Journal of the Louisiana Historical Association

Image Sources

[1] Greg Willis, CC BY-SA 2.0 <https://creativecommons.org/licenses/by-sa/2.0>, via Wikimedia Commons https://commons.wikimedia.org/wiki/File:Voodoo_Altar_New_Orleans.jpg

[2] https://commons.wikimedia.org/wiki/File:The_Complexity_of_a_Nebula_-_NGC_5189_(27747553890).jpg

[3] Jeremy Burgin, CC BY 2.0 <https://creativecommons.org/licenses/by/2.0>, via Wikimedia Commons https://upload.wikimedia.org/wikipedia/commons/7/79/Voodoo_altar_in_Tropenmuseum.jpg

[4] Wayne S. Grazio, CC BY-NC-ND 2.0 DEED < https://creativecommons.org/licenses/by-nc-nd/2.0/> https://www.flickr.com/photos/fotograzio/17993185248

[5] fenixcs, CC BY-NC-ND 2.0 DEED < https://creativecommons.org/licenses/by-nc-nd/2.0/ > https://www.flickr.com/photos/fenixcsmar/30208171733

[6] Jeremy Burgin, CC BY-SA 2.0 <https://creativecommons.org/licenses/by-sa/2.0>, via Wikimedia Commons https://commons.wikimedia.org/wiki/File:Statue-of-Legba-by-Jeremy-Burgin.jpg

[7] Sam Fentress, CC BY-SA 2.0 <https://creativecommons.org/licenses/by-sa/2.0>, via Wikimedia Commons https://commons.wikimedia.org/wiki/File:VoodooValris.jpg

[8] https://commons.wikimedia.org/wiki/File:Damballah_La_Flambeau.jpg

[9] https://commons.wikimedia.org/wiki/File:VeveAyizan.svg

[10] Nicolas Munoz, CC BY-NC-SA 2.0 DEED < https://creativecommons.org/licenses/by-nc-sa/2.0/ > https://www.flickr.com/photos/nicolasmunoz/5817315380

[11] Calvin Hennick, for WBUR Boston, CC BY 3.0 <https://creativecommons.org/licenses/by/3.0>, via Wikimedia Commons https://commons.wikimedia.org/wiki/File:Haitian_vodou_altar_to_Petwo,_Rada,_and_Gede_spirits;_November_5,_2010..jpg

[12] Teogomez, CC BY-SA 3.0 <http://creativecommons.org/licenses/by-sa/3.0/>, via Wikimedia Commons https://commons.wikimedia.org/wiki/File:Grisgristuareg.JPG

[13] Hidrash, CC BY-SA 4.0 <https://creativecommons.org/licenses/by-sa/4.0>, via Wikimedia Commons https://commons.wikimedia.org/wiki/File:A_man_dancing_the_Jars_dance_in_Tamale,_Ghana.jpg

[14] https://unsplash.com/photos/ZlIIA-4sGXU

[15] https://www.flickr.com/photos/edk7/51102873969

[16] https://www.flickr.com/photos/wcouch/3464210637

[17] https://unsplash.com/photos/iSGbjKZ9erg

[18] https://unsplash.com/photos/iSyyY1GfYSw

[19] https://pixabay.com/es/illustrations/meditaci%C3%B3n-reflexi%C3%B3n-universo-5286678/

[20] https://www.pexels.com/photo/black-gold-14704594/

[21] https://www.pxfuel.com/en/free-photo-oesnm

[22] https://creazilla.com/nodes/1675858-serpent-snake-woman-illustration

[23] https://unsplash.com/photos/hMYAVaOWSHc

[24] https://www.flickr.com/photos/mark-gunn/39651373500

[25] https://www.flickr.com/photos/africa-rising/26226168738

[26] https://www.flickr.com/photos/59489479@N08/17940796562

www.ingramcontent.com/pod-product-compliance
Lightning Source LLC
Chambersburg PA
CBHW072156200426
43209CB00052B/1271